The Vegetarian Microwave Cookbook

Carol Bowen has a degree in Home Economics from the University of Surrey. She has been a freelance cookery writer, food consultant and broadcaster since 1979, having previously worked for *Good Housekeeping*, *Homes & Gardens* and Birds Eye (as Head of Consumer Affairs). Carol has contributed frequently to national newspapers, magazines and radio programmes including a regular spot with Michael Aspel on Capital Radio and a cookery programme 'What's Cooking' on Piccadilly Radio in Manchester. On television she was cookery consultant and guest on the *X-Cel Diet* for TV AM with Diana Dors and made a guest appearance on the BBC's 'Snowdon on Camera' on food photography. To date she has written over forty cookery books including *Versatile Vegetables* (Octopus) which won the 1984 Bejam Cookery Book of the Year Award. She has a strong belief in and a passion for the microwave – a subject on which she advises the *Sunday Telegraph Magazine*. Carol Bowen is married and lives with her husband and two children in Surrey.

D1439900

Other cookery books available in Pan

Carol Bowen

The Vegetarian Microwave Cookbook

Pan Original
Pan Books London, Sydney and Auckland

First published 1988 by Pan Books Ltd, Cavaye Place,
London SW10 9PG
9 8 7 6 5 4 3 2 1
© Carol Bowen 1988
ISBN 0 330 30187 X

Phototypeset by Input Typesetting Ltd, London
Printed in Great Britain by Richard Clay Limited

Contents

Acknowledgements

I should like to offer my grateful thanks to Sharp Electronics (UK), Thorn EMI Domestic Appliances and Robert Bosch Ltd for kindly supplying the ovens on which all testing was done for this book.

For information thanks to the California Raisin Advisory Board, Danish Agricultural Producers, W. Jordan (Cereals) Ltd, Colman's Kitchen, The Banana Fruit Service, Food and Wine From France Ltd, Flour Advisory Bureau, Tabasco Hot Line, Danish Dairy Board, H. J. Heinz Co. Ltd, CMA (UK), Billingtons, Mushroom Growers' Association, Outspan, Dutch Dairy Bureau, Gales, Pasta Information Centre and Weetabix Ltd.

I dedicate this book to my first ever cookery teacher Mrs Green who taught me to cook not only with my hands but eyes, nose and, of course, taste buds.

It is also for my husband, Peter, without whose sustained support it could never have been written.

I also wish to thank my helpers and friends Nanny Elizabeth Kempton and Carol Hawkins.

Foreword

I wish that I could say I am vegetarian of many years' standing but sadly it is only recently that I have been able to boast the merits of vegetarian cuisine. Today I try to convince anyone within earshot the delights of eating no or less meat, poultry, fish and game and love to sing the delights of healthy meals based on wholegrains, pulses, pasta, vegetables, seeds and, still my first love, fruits.

The changeover to a more vegetarian-based diet however did not come suddenly – I did find I had to gradually wean myself, and my family, from the traditional meat and two vegetable meals they had come to expect and like. Why change then, you may ask? Mainly for dietary reasons is my reply. Faced with bringing up and feeding two young children, for whom I wanted to have the very best start in life, I felt I needed to reassess our eating habits (especially in the light of reports on poor nutrition with children of school age and younger). Luckily they found the slight changeover easier to come to terms with than my husband and myself – what you have never had you never miss, I suppose.

During this time the biggest asset in the kitchen was my microwave (the food processor was a great help too). It really did make short cuts on all those lengthy cooking processes that often discourage a vegetarian cook. I can boast many years' experiences with the microwave oven – I first dabbled with its delights back in 1972 and have been a convert ever since. These two methods of cooking – with the microwave and with vegetarian foods – are naturals together.

In the writing of this book I have endeavoured to create recipes that will be welcomed by established vegetarians and would-be non-meat eating folk alike. They are backed up by a brief but comprehensive introduction to the microwave itself so that you get the best from both worlds. I hope after sampling you'll agree with me that the marrying of high technology with health is the best thing to come out of the kitchen for years!

CAROL BOWEN

Introduction

The microwave is undoubtedly a great bonus to the vegetarian or non-meat eating cook. It will quickly and efficiently cook wholegrains, vegetables, fruits, pasta, rice and other vegetarian-based foods like eggs and cheese in a fraction of the time it would take to cook conventionally.

The microwave will also help to eliminate some of those lengthy pre-preparation processes, like soaking of dried peas, beans and lentils and rehydration of dried fruits – upon which many main course vegetarian meals are based. In essence the microwave promotes a healthy non-meat eating or vegetarian pattern of eating and cooking.

Like many appliances there are however a few dishes that it does not cook as well as the conventional oven or grill and some dishes that it cooks infinitely better. Throughout the writing of this book, and certainly in the recipe selection, the merits of the microwave have been borne in mind. You will therefore find recipes in the sections that follow that boast the advantages of the microwave – and those that do not have been left for other methods of cooking.

It has been assumed throughout that the vegetarian reader will eat dairy produce like cheese, eggs, yogurt, butter and cream – although a strictly vegan section has also been incorporated (and the committed vegan will also find recipes in many of the other chapters of the book). Powdered gelatine, made from animal origins, has also been quoted, with an alternative of vegetable agar-agar. Wherever possible healthy wholegrains and unadulterated products have also been used since these generally promote good health.

On the question of good health the microwave repeatedly wins hands down on any other kitchen appliance – since without any contrived or forced effect it is possible to use less fat, less liquid, less salt and fewer flavour-promoting agents in basic everyday cooking due to its individual and specialist cooking action.

Microwave Master Class

Many basic microwave cookery books cover the theory and principles of microwave cooking in detail. Established microwave cooks will already have grasped the differences between microwave cooking and conventional cooking. If you are a would-be microwave cook, a novice in microwave cookery or an established user who isn't getting the best from their microwave then consider the following condensed, brief explanation of microwave cooking – the microwave master class:

Cooking by Microwave

Microwave cooking is cooking by electromagnetic waves that travel at high speed into food via the magnetron in a microwave oven. Microwaves are absorbed by the moisture molecules within food, causing them to vibrate rapidly, producing heat to cook food. This vibration happens many thousands of times per second and explains the speed of microwave cooking. Microwaves are absorbed by food but are reflected by metals (which is why they are safely contained within the oven cavity and why metal cannot be used as a cooking utensil) and can pass through materials like glass, china, paper, pottery and most plastics (which is why they make ideal cooking containers).

Microwaves generally do not brown food over short periods of time and cannot be used for shallow or deep frying (although a microwave browning dish will reproduce a browned or seared shallow frying effect with great success). They will cook vegetables, fruits, grains, pasta, eggs and cheese remarkably well (although time savings vary from food to food), but cannot be used to boil eggs and produce crisp batter mixtures like Yorkshire puddings. Crisp batter products can however be made if your oven is one of the new generation combination ovens that uses forced-air convection with microwave.

Microwave Power Level Controls

Most modern day microwave ovens have more than one power level control although early models simply worked on full (100%) power. Today the very simplest have at least 3 power levels – a full (100%) level; 50% (medium) level; and 20% (defrost) level. Others have up to 10 levels with a numerical calibration; a descriptive guide from say 'keep warm' to 'fast cook'; or special manufacturer's description that corresponds with their handbook or manual. Whatever the power level guide given on your microwave all of the recipes in this book can be cooked with success. Simply follow the chart and guide on pages 40–1 for specific details.

Microwave Cooking Techniques

Many of the techniques employed in conventional cooking like stirring, turning over and rearranging are also used in microwave cooking. However, since microwaves cook extra fast, their importance is more critical in achieving good results. The following techniques, factors and tips all have a part to play in cooking the microwave way:

Covering – many recipes call for a food to be covered during microwave cooking. In many cases this is to help speed up cooking times by trapping steam within food but may also be employed to prevent drying out. Cover with the lid to a dish, a plate or saucer, greaseproof paper or absorbent kitchen towel. Remember when removing any cover that steam will have been trapped so take care to prevent burning yourself. If cook bags have been used then prick in several places with scissors to prevent a ballooning effect.

2

Stirring – microwaves penetrate to a depth of about 5cm/ 2 in into food (dispelling the myth that they cook from the inside out!) and therefore food must be stirred from the outside of the dish to the inside to ensure even cooking or heating. Usually this is only necessary once, about halfway through the cooking time but always follow specific recipe instructions for best results.

Turning over, rearranging and rotating – these are other procedures used to ensure food cooks evenly and are employed when a food cannot be stirred. A recipe may ask for an item to be turned over once or several times during cooking; rearranged in the oven so that hot spot effects are eliminated; or the dish rotated at regular intervals if your model of microwave does not have a turntable.

Arranging – successful microwave cooking depends also upon the way foods are arranged in the microwave for even absorption of energy. One of the following ways may be employed:

- items that are similar in size, composition and density, like jacket potatoes, should be arranged in a ring pattern so that they receive equal amounts of energy.
- items of uneven or irregular shape should be arranged so that the thicker portions are positioned to the outer edge of the dish where they will receive more energy, e.g. broccoli spears.
- if cooking a plated meal then place foods with a denser or thicker nature to the outer edge of the plate, leaving the centre for more fragile, porous and temperature-sensitive foods.
- wherever possible ensure that foods are of an even depth – if this is not possible then rearrange once or twice to compensate.
- cook wherever possible in round dishes for even results. If oval or loaf-shaped dishes are used then shield the ends for part of the cooking time.

Shielding – this is a technique used to prevent overcooking of sensitive areas of food. Usually thin pieces of metal foil are used to cover these areas for part of the cooking time – thereby reducing the amount of total energy they receive. It is the only time when small pieces of metal may be introduced into the microwave and should always be checked and positioned so that they never touch the oven walls or arcing may occur.

Releasing pressure – many foods have a tight membrane surrounding their flesh like potatoes, tomatoes and aubergines. These could burst during the high speed cooking associated with the microwave. It is therefore suggested that such foods are pricked with a fork prior to cooking to eliminate this effect. The same has to be said for boil-in-the-bag pouches and polythene cook bags.

Observing standing times – after a food has reached the end of the required cooking time (and the oven has automatically switched off) it will continue to cook by the conducted heat still trapped in the food. To ensure that a food does not overcook with this 'additional' energy effect standing times of a few minutes should be observed. In most cases this is only 2–3 minutes, as in vegetables, fruits and pasta or rice dishes but can be up to 15 minutes for baked items and dense nut and vegetable roasts.

Factors affecting Microwave Cooking

Density – the denser the food the longer it will take to cook.

Quantity – the more food the longer it will take to cook. Timing of items relate directly to quantity. Usually when doubling the amount of food increase the cooking time by one third to one half, and if reducing the quantity by half then reduce the time by less than one half.

Composition – fats and sugars attract microwave energy faster than water-based products so high sugar and high fat items will generally cook faster. High water items, such as vegetables, cook slower than low water foods like cakes and breads which cook very fast.

Shape – regular-shaped foods cook better, faster and more evenly than irregular-shaped foods. Wherever possible try to cook foods of uniform shape or shield thin areas with small pieces of foil.

4

Microwave Cookware and Utensils

With the exception of metal, which cannot be used for microwave cooking, the range of equipment that can be used in the microwave is more extensive than that used in conventional cooking. China, pottery and glass can all be used with great success – but do check that they do not have a metallic trim or metal signature on their base. Pottery should be of the non-porous kind except for chicken bricks (which can be soaked for 15 minutes and then used according to manufacturer's instructions).

For short cooking operations where temperatures are not excessively high then paper cookware, plastic cookware, greaseproof paper, absorbent kitchen towel, cardboard boxes, paper napkins and straw or wicker baskets may be used.

Microwave polythene cook bags and or roaster bags are also good for general use but remember to replace any metal ties with string, elastic bands or plastic ties (although many manufacturers are now replacing the traditional metal ties with plastic for the microwave cook).

Never use metal cookware or baking tins, dishes with 'hidden' cast-iron bases, plates with metal decorative trims, lead crystal, bottles with narrow necks (any build up of pressure can cause the container to explode) or melamine plastics (which tend to char and burn).

In addition to these general household basics there are a whole host of special microwave dishes, utensils and gadgets all designed to promote good microwave cooking results. These include browning dishes, special defrost boxes, special plastic microwave cookware in the traditional shapes and sizes of metal bakeware, roasting and baking trivets and microwave thermometers and probes. A browning dish is a very useful microwave extra since it really does duplicate the browning process associated with conventionally cooked food. It is a dish made of a glass ceramic substance that has a special coating that attracts microwave energy. After preheating, usually at 100%

(high) power for about 6 minutes, it browns foods and will simulate a shallow-fried effect on items like eggs. The dish does become very hot so oven gloves should always be used when handling.

If in doubt it is possible to test whether a dish is suitable for microwave use or not. Simply place 250ml/8fl oz cold water in a glass jug in the dish to be checked. Microwave at 100% (high) for 1 minute. If the water becomes hot the dish can be used – if the dish becomes hot it is unsuitable.

All Eyes on the Food

Your microwave will bring you countless advantages in cooking – it will bring you speedily cooked food at reduced energy costs. It will cook food efficiently in a cooler environment without excess cooking smells and odours. Invariably it will reduce washing up since you can cook and serve in the same dish and all the nutritional value of the food being cooked is likely to be retained. It is a safe appliance (with only minimal supervision) for the elderly, infirm, disabled and young and is safe for quick defrosting and reheating.

Portable models are especially useful since they can be moved from room to room as required; taken outdoors onto the patio or terrace to boost the barbecue with alfresco entertaining; and can be taken away to the coast, holiday home or caravan to help with no-fuss meals.

I have found them to be a bonus when bottle-feeding infants since they reheat chilled bottles of baby milk to drinking temperature in seconds. They have also been proven to be a godsend when a well-meaning crowd arrives just in time for supper!

These advantages acknowledged, care and respect should still be exercised with the microwave. All ovens are different, even of the same make, and performances will therefore vary slightly. Take time to get to know your oven and its qualities but moreover rely upon your own senses for guidance. Your eyes, nose and fingers should still be used to check if a food is cooking well – use them to judge each stage of a recipe before going on to the next. When in doubt refer back to your microwave handbook, the recipe guidelines and method and err on the side of safety by under- rather than over-cooking. Time can always be added but never taken away.

In general I have found that cakes and sponge type puddings often appear 'wet' on the surface when cooked but will dry out when standing times are observed. Test by inserting a wooden cocktail stick at the minimum time stated – the mixture will be cooked if the stick comes out clean. Custards, quiches and egg based fillings may also appear wet or soft in the centre when cooked but will firm up upon standing. Insert a knife near to the centre to check if cooked – if it comes out clean it is. Vegetables are usually cooked when just fork-tender or tender crisp and soften further upon standing. Pastries are cooked when the base is dry and opaque. Reheated plated meals are ready to serve when the base of the plate feels hot to the touch – about 2–3 minutes at 100% (high).

A Final Word on Safety

Always disconnect your cooker from its electrical supply before cleaning. Ensure door seals are free from dust, grease and general food debris by regularly cleaning. Choose an oven, if you are a would-be buyer or replacement buyer, from a retailer with a good after-sales service or take out a good service contract to cover parts and cost. Never use your oven if you think it may be damaged in any way at all – call in a reputable service engineer at once. Finally, after your guarantee period is over, consider seriously a yearly maintenance check for oven efficiency and safety.

A–Z of Vegetarian Foods in the Microwave

A

Aduki Beans

TO COOK SOAKED BEANS Place soaked beans in a cooking dish. Cover with boiling water. Cover and cook for the 1st time and power specified. Reduce the power setting and cook for the 2nd time specified, adding extra boiling water to cover if needed. Drain to use as required.

Quantity soaked beans	1st Time/Power	2nd Time/Power
225g/8oz	10 minutes/ 100% (high)	10–15 minutes/ 50% (medium)

(See page 16 for instructions on soaking dried beans.)

Almonds

TO BLANCH Pour water over almonds and cook, uncovered, for time specified. Drain and remove skins. Leave to dry on absorbent kitchen towel.

Quantity	Water	Power	Minutes
100g/4oz	250ml/8fl oz	100% (high)	1

TO BROWN Place almonds on a large flat dish. Cook for time specified, stirring every 1 minute. Allow to cool.

Quantity	Power	Minutes
25–50g/1–2oz whole	100% (high)	5–6
25–50g/1–2oz flaked	100% (high)	3–5

B

Baked Beans

TO COOK BAKED BEANS IN TOMATO SAUCE, CURRIED BEANS, CASSOULET BEANS, CHILLI BEANS, BEANS IN SWEET AND SOUR SAUCE AND BARBECUE BEANS Place in a bowl, cover and cook for the time specified, stirring once.

Quantity	Power	Minutes
1 × 142g/5oz can	100% (high)	1¼–1½
1 × 220g/7¾oz can	100% (high)	1½–2
1 × 447g/15¾oz can	100% (high)	2½–3

Barley

POT BARLEY Toast if liked. Place in a large cooking dish with boiling water. Cover loosely with a lid or vented cling film and cook for 1st time and power specified. Reduce power setting and cook for 2nd time specified, stirring 3 times. Leave to stand, covered, for 5–10 minutes before serving. Fluff with a fork to separate the grains to serve.

Quantity	Water	Salt	1st Time/Power	2nd Time/Power
175g/6oz	1 litre/1¾ pints	1 tsp	3 minutes/ 100% (high)	40 minutes/ 50% (medium)

Black Beans

TO COOK SOAKED BEANS Place soaked beans in a cooking dish. Cover with boiling water. Cover and cook for the 1st time and power specified. Reduce the power setting and cook for the 2nd time specified, adding extra boiling water to cover if needed. Drain to use as required.

Quantity soaked beans	1st Time/Power	2nd Time/Power
225g/8oz	10 minutes/	20–25 minutes/
	100% (high)	50% (medium)

(See page 16 for instructions on soaking dried beans.)

Black-eyed Beans

TO COOK SOAKED BEANS   Place soaked beans in a cooking dish. Cover with boiling water. Cover and cook for the 1st time and power specified. Reduce the power setting and cook for the 2nd time specified, adding extra boiling water to cover if needed. Drain to use as required.

Quantity soaked beans	1st Time/Power	2nd Time/Power
225g/8oz	10 minutes/	10–15 minutes/
	100% (high)	50% (medium)

(See page 16 for instructions on soaking dried beans.)

Bread

TO COOK BASIC WHITE OR WHOLEMEAL   Mix 1 tsp sugar with 1 tsp dried yeast and 150ml/¼ pint warm water in a jug. Leave until frothy, about 10–15 minutes. Sift 450g/1lb plain or plain wholemeal flour with ½ tsp salt into a bowl. Cook at 100% (high) for ½ minute to warm. Rub in 40g/1½oz butter for white bread and 15g/½oz butter for wholemeal bread. Add the yeast liquid and 150ml/¼ pint warm water and mix to a pliable dough. Knead on a lightly floured surface until smooth and elastic, about 5 minutes. Prove the dough until doubled in size (see PROVING DOUGH page 24). Knead again for 2–3 minutes, shape and place in a 900g/2lb loaf dish. Prove again until doubled in size. Lightly brush with oil and sprinkle with nuts, seeds or bran. Cook for the time specified, giving the dish a half turn 3 times. Leave to stand for 5 minutes before turning out to cool. Brown under a preheated hot grill if liked.

Quantity	Power	Minutes
1 × 900g/2lb loaf	100% (high)	6

FROZEN LARGE WHITE OR BROWN SLICED OR UNCUT LOAF To thaw, loosen wrapper but do not remove. Cook for the time specified. Leave to stand for 5 minutes before slicing or removing ready-cut slices. Leave a further 10 minutes before serving.

Quantity	Power	Minutes
1 × 800g/1¾lb	20% (defrost)	4

FROZEN INDIVIDUAL BREAD SLICES AND ROLLS To thaw, wrap loosely in absorbent kitchen towel and cook for the time specified. Leave to stand for 2 minutes before serving.

Quantity	Power	Minutes
1 slice/1 roll	20% (defrost)	¼–½
2 slices/2 rolls	20% (defrost)	½–1
4 slices/4 rolls	20% (defrost)	1½–2

FROZEN PITTA BREAD To thaw, place on a double thickness piece of absorbent kitchen towel and cook for the time specified, turning once.

Quantity	Power	Minutes
2	20% (defrost)	1½–2
4	20% (defrost)	2–3

FROZEN CRUMPETS To thaw and reheat, place on a double thickness sheet of absorbent kitchen towel and cook for the time specified, turning once.

Quantity	Power	Minutes
2	100% (high)	½–¾
4	100% (high)	1–1½

12

Broad Beans (dried)

TO COOK SOAKED BEANS Place soaked beans in a cooking dish. Cover with boiling water. Cover and cook for the 1st time and power specified. Reduce the power setting and cook for the 2nd time specified, adding extra boiling water to cover if needed. Drain to use as required.

Quantity	1st Time/Power	2nd Time/Power
225g/8oz	10 minutes/ 100% (high)	20–25 minutes/ 50% (medium)

(See page 16 for instructions on soaking dried beans.)

Buckwheat

PRE-ROASTED Place in a large cooking dish with boiling water and salt. Cover loosely with a lid or vented cling film and cook for 1st time and power specified. Reduce power setting and cook for 2nd time specified, stirring 2–3 times. Leave to stand, covered, for 3–5 minutes before serving. Fluff with a fork to separate to serve.

Quantity	Water	Salt	1st Time/Power	2nd Time/Power
175g/6oz	600ml/1 pint	1 tsp	3 minutes/ 100% (high)	12 minutes/ 50% (medium)

Bulghur

BULGHUR GRAINS (CRACKED WHEAT) Place in a large cooking dish with boiling water and salt. Cover loosely with a lid or vented cling film and cook for 1st time and power specified. Reduce power setting and cook for 2nd time specified, stirring twice. Leave to stand, covered, for 3–5 minutes before serving. Fluff the grains with a fork to separate to serve.

Quantity	Water	Salt	1st Time/Power	2nd Time/Power
225g/8oz	500ml/18fl oz	1 tsp	3 minutes/ 100% (high)	9–12 minutes/ 50% (medium)

Butter or Lima Beans (dried)

TO COOK SOAKED BEANS   Place soaked beans in a cooking
dish. Cover with boiling water. Cover and cook for the 1st
time and power specified. Reduce the power setting and
cook for the 2nd time specified, adding extra boiling water
to cover if needed. Drain to use as required.

Quantity soaked beans	1st Time/Power	2nd Time/Power
225g/8oz	10 minutes/	20–25 minutes/
	100% (high)	50% (medium)

(See page 16 for instructions on soaking dried beans.)

C

Cannellini Beans (dried)

TO COOK SOAKED BEANS   Place soaked beans in a cooking
dish. Cover with boiling water. Cover and cook for the 1st
time and power specified. Reduce the power setting and
cook for the 2nd time specified, adding extra boiling water
to cover if needed. Drain to use as required.

Quantity soaked beans	1st Time/Power	2nd Time/Power
225g/8oz	10 minutes/	20–25 minutes/
	100% (high)	50% (medium)

(See page 16 for instructions on soaking dried beans.)

Cheese

TO RIPEN SEMI-SOFT CHEESES   Place on serving dish and cook
for time specified depending upon degree of ripeness,
checking constantly and turn after half of the time. Leave
to stand for 5 minutes before serving.

Quantity	Power	Seconds
225g/8oz	30% (low)	15–45

TO SOFTEN CHILLED HARD CHEESES Place on a serving dish and cook for time specified, turning over after half of the time. Leave to stand for 5 minutes before serving.

Quantity	Power	Seconds
225g/8oz	30% (low)	30–45

Chick Peas

TO COOK SOAKED PEAS Place soaked peas in a cooking dish. Cover with boiling water. Cover and cook for the 1st time and power specified. Reduce the power setting and cook for the 2nd time specified, adding extra boiling water to cover if needed. Drain to use as required.

Quantity	1st Time/Power	2nd Time/Power
225g/8oz	10 minutes/ 100% (high)	20–25 minutes/ 50% (medium)

(See page 16 for instructions on soaking dried beans.)

Coconut

TO TOAST Spread the desiccated coconut on a plate. Cook for the time specified, stirring every 1 minute until golden. Allow to cool before using.

Quantity	Power	Minutes
100g/4oz	100% (high)	5–6

Cottage Cheese

FRESH TO MAKE Place the milk in a bowl and cook, uncovered, for the 1st time and power specified. Stir in the rennet and cook for the 2nd time specified or until the milk has set. Stir to separate the curds from the whey. Place in a muslin-lined sieve, tie to enclose and suspend to drain overnight. Season or flavour the cottage cheese as liked. Makes about 100g/3½oz.

Quantity milk	Rennet	1st Time/Power	2nd Time/Power
600ml/1 pint	1½ tbsp	1½–2 minutes/ 100% (high)	4–5 minutes/ 30% (low)

Couscous

PRE-COOKED Place in a cooking dish with warm water. Leave to soak for 10 minutes. Add butter and salt to taste. Cook for time specified, stirring every 3–4 minutes. Leave to stand, covered, for 2–3 minutes before serving.

Quantity	Water	Butter	Power	Minutes
350g/12oz	250ml/8fl oz	50g/2oz	50% (medium)	15

D

Dried Beans

TO HASTEN SOAKING PRIOR TO COOKING Place in a cooking dish. Cover with boiling water. Cover and cook for 5 minutes at 100% (high). Leave to stand for 1½ hours before draining and rinsing to cook.

Dried Fruit Salad

Place in a dish with fruit juice and water. Cover and cook for 1st time specified, stirring twice. Leave to stand and cool for 1 hour. Stir in sugar and cook for 2nd time specified. Serve warm or chilled.

Quantity	Fruit Juice	Water	Power	1st Time	Sugar	2nd Time
450g/1lb	600ml/ 1 pint	600ml/ 1 pint	100% (high)	10 minutes	75g/3oz	6 minutes

F

Flageolet Beans (dried)

TO COOK SOAKED BEANS Place soaked beans in a cooking dish. Cover with boiling water. Cover and cook for the 1st time and power specified. Reduce the power setting and cook for the 2nd time specified, adding extra boiling water to cover if needed. Drain to use as required.

Quantity soaked beans	1st Time/Power	2nd Time/Power
225g/8oz	10 minutes/ 100% (high)	20–25 minutes/ 50% (medium)

(See page 16 for instructions on soaking dried beans.)

Ful Medame Beans

TO COOK SOAKED BEANS Place soaked beans in a cooking dish. Cover with boiling water. Cover and cook for the 1st time and power specified. Reduce the power setting and cook for the 2nd time specified, adding extra boiling water to cover if needed. Drain to use as required.

Quantity soaked beans	1st Time/Power	2nd Time/Power
225g/8oz	10 minutes/ 100% (high)	20–25 minutes/ 50% (medium)

(See page 16 for instructions on soaking dried beans.)

G

Green Peas (whole dried)

TO COOK SOAKED PEAS Place soaked peas in a cooking dish. Cover with boiling water. Cover and cook for the 1st time and power specified. Reduce the power setting and cook for the 2nd time specified, adding extra boiling water to cover if needed. Drain to use as required.

Quantity soaked peas	1st Time/Power	2nd Time/Power
225g/8oz	10 minutes/	10–15 minutes/
	100% (high)	50% (medium)

(See page 16 for instructions on soaking dried beans.)

H

Haricot Beans

TO COOK SOAKED BEANS Place soaked beans in a cooking dish. Cover with boiling water. Cover and cook for the 1st time and power specified. Reduce the power setting and cook for the 2nd time specified, adding extra boiling water to cover if needed. Drain to use as required.

Quantity soaked beans	1st Time/Power	2nd Time/Power
225g/8oz	10 minutes/	20–25 minutes/
	100% (high)	50% (medium)

(See page 16 for instructions on soaking dried beans.)

Hazelnuts

TO TOAST AND SKIN Place hazelnuts on a large flat dish. Cook for time specified, stirring twice. Rub in a cloth to remove the skins.

Quantity	Power	Minutes
25–50g/1–2oz	100% (high)	2–2½

Herbs (fresh)

TO DRY Trim and sort, wash and dry and measure loosely packed in a measuring jug. Spread on absorbent kitchen towel in a single layer. Place in the microwave with a small glass of water and cook for the time specified, stirring and rearranging every 2 minutes. Dry on fresh kitchen towel until cool then crumble to store in airtight jars. Store for 3–6 months in a cool, dry, dark place.

Quantity	Power	Minutes
300ml/½ pint	100% (high)	7–9

Honey

TO SOFTEN OR MELT/REVITALIZE CRYSTALLIZED OR HARDENED Place honey in a bowl or leave in a jar and cook for the time specified, stirring once.

Quantity	Power	Time
2 tbsp	100% (high)	10 seconds
1 × 450g/1lb jar	100% (high)	1½–2 minutes

L

Lentils

TO COOK Place in a large dish with a little chopped onion, celery and lemon juice. Cover with boiling water or stock, add salt and pepper to taste. Cover and cook for the time specified, stirring once. Time cooking according to end use.

Quantity	Water	Power	Minutes
225g/8oz	900ml/1½ pints	100% (high)	20–25

M

Mayonnaise

Beat the egg yolks (at room temperature) with a little salt, mustard powder, cayenne pepper and the lemon juice or wine vinegar. Place the oil in a jug and cook for the time specified. Slowly whisk the oil, drop by drop, into the egg mixture until it starts to thicken then add in a thin steady stream.

Alternatively, place egg mixture in a blender and, with the motor running, add the oil in a thin steady stream and blend until thick and glossy.

Quantity egg yolks	Lemon juice/ vinegar	Oil	Power	Seconds
3	5 tsp	300 ml/½ pint	100% (high)	30

Millet

MILLET GRAINS   Toast if liked. Place in a large cooking dish with boiling water. Cover loosely with a lid or vented cling film and cook for 1st time and power specified. Reduce power setting and cook for 2nd time specified, stirring twice. Leave to stand, covered, for 3–5 minutes before serving. Fluff with a fork to separate the grains to serve.

Quantity	Water	Salt	1st Time/Power	2nd Time/Power
225g/8oz	650ml/22fl oz	1 tsp	3 minutes/ 100% (high)	12 minutes/ 50% (medium)

Mung Beans

TO COOK SOAKED BEANS   Place soaked beans in a cooking dish. Cover with boiling water. Cover and cook for the 1st time and power specified. Reduce the power setting and cook for the 2nd time specified, adding extra boiling water to cover if needed. Drain to use as required.

Quantity soaked beans	1st Time/Power	2nd Time/Power
225g/8oz	10 minutes/ 100% (high)	10–15 minutes/ 50% (medium)

(See page 16 for instructions on soaking dried beans.)

O

Oats

OAT GRAINS   Toast if liked. Place in a large cooking dish with boiling water and salt. Cover loosely with a lid or vented cling film and cook for 1st time and power specified. Reduce power setting and cook for 2nd time specified, stirring twice. Leave to stand, covered, for 5–10 minutes before serving. Fluff the grains with a fork to separate to serve.

Quantity	Water	Salt	1st Time/Power	2nd Time/Power
175g/6oz	750ml/ 1¼ pints	1 tsp	3 minutes/ 100% (high)	20–22 minutes/ 50% (medium)

P

Pasta

PRE-COOKING LASAGNE FOR LAYERING WITH SAVOURY MIXTURE   Place lasagne in a large rectangular dish with the boiling water and a pinch of salt. Cover and cook for the time specified, rearranging the sheets once. Drain and rinse under cold running water to use.

Quantity	Water	Power	Minutes
225g/8oz	750ml/1¼ pints	100% (high)	7–9

PRE-COOKING CANNELLONI FOR STUFFING   Place the cannelloni in a dish and add the water and a pinch of salt. Cover and cook for the time specified. Leave to stand for 5 minutes then drain and stuff and cover with chosen sauce.

Quantity	Water	Power	Minutes
225g/8oz	750ml/1¼ pints	100% (high)	1

FRESH PASTA (ALL TYPES)   Place pasta in a large dish with a little oil and the boiling water. Cover and cook for the time specified. Drain and use as required.

Quantity	Boiling water	Power	Minutes
225g/8oz	750ml/1¼ pints	100% (high)	2–3

COOKING CANNED PASTA   Place canned pasta (macaroni cheese, ravioli in tomato sauce, spaghetti in tomato sauce or pasta shapes in sauce, for example) in a bowl, cover and cook for the time specified, stirring once.

Quantity	Power	Minutes
1 × 213g/7½oz can	100% (high)	1½–2
1 × 397g/14oz can	100% (high)	2½–3
1 × 425g/15oz can	100% (high)	2½–3

DRIED PASTA   Place the pasta in a large bowl with the boiling water and a little oil. Cook for the time specified, stirring once. Leave to stand for 3–5 minutes before draining to serve.

Quantity/type pasta	Water	Power	Minutes
225g/8oz egg noodles and tagliatelle	1.2 litres/2 pints	100% (high)	6
225g/8oz short-cut macaroni	1.2 lites/2 pints	100% (high)	10
225g/8oz pasta shells and shapes	1.2 litres/2 pints	100% (high)	12–14
225g/8oz spaghetti	1.2 litres/2 pints	100% (high)	10–12
225g/8oz ravioli	1.5 litres/2½ pints	100% (high)	10

FROZEN COOKED PASTA To thaw and reheat, place in a dish, cover and cook for the time specified, stirring twice.

Quantity	Power	Minutes
275g/10oz	20% (defrost)	10

Peanuts

TO ROAST Place shelled, husked raw nuts on a large shallow plate. Add the oil and toss to coat. Cook for the time specified, stirring and turning twice. Allow to cool on absorbent kitchen towel. Season with salt if liked.

Quantity	Oil	Power	Minutes
150g/5oz	1 tsp	100% (high)	5–7

Pinto Beans

TO COOK SOAKED BEANS Place soaked beans in a cooking dish. Cover with boiling water. Cover and cook for the 1st time and power specified. Reduce the power setting and cook for the 2nd time specified, adding extra boiling water to cover if needed. Drain to use as required.

Quantity soaked beans	1st Time/Power	2nd Time/Power
225g/8oz	10 minutes/ 100% (high)	10–15 minutes/ 50% (medium)

(See page 16 for instructions on soaking dried beans.)

Porridge

TRADITIONAL OATMEAL Place the oatmeal, salt and water or milk in a bowl, mixing well. Cover with vented cling film and cook for the time specified, stirring twice. Leave to stand, covered, for 2 minutes before serving.

Quantity	Salt	Water/Milk	Power	Minutes
30g/1¼oz (to serve 1)	¼ tsp	175ml/6fl oz	30% (low)	10–12
65g/2½oz (to serve 2)	½ tsp	350ml/12fl oz	30% (low)	10–12
125g/4½oz (to serve 4)	¾ tsp	750ml/1¼ pints	30% (low)	12–14

QUICK-COOK OATMEAL Place the oatmeal, salt and water or milk in a bowl, mixing well. Cover with vented cling film and cook for the time specified, stirring twice. Leave to stand, covered, for 2 minutes before serving.

Quantity	Salt	Water/Milk	Power	Minutes
30g/1¼oz (to serve 1)	¼ tsp	175ml/6fl oz	30% (low)	5
65g/2½oz (to serve 2)	½ tsp	350ml/12fl oz	30% (low)	5–6
125g/4½oz (to serve 4)	¾ tsp	750ml/1¼ pints	30% (low)	7–8

Proving Dough

Bread dough proving can be hastened using the microwave. Simply give the dough a short burst of energy during the rising process then leave to stand for 5–10 minutes before repeating until the dough has risen sufficiently. It is suggested that a burst of energy at 100% (high) power for 5–10 seconds is ideal for proving a 900g/2lb piece of dough.

R

Red Kidney Beans (dried)

TO COOK SOAKED BEANS Place soaked beans in a cooking dish. Cover with boiling water. Cover and cook for the 1st time and power specified. Reduce the power setting and cook for the 2nd time specified, adding extra boiling water to cover if needed. Drain to use as required.

Quantity soaked beans	1st Time/Power	2nd Time/Power
225g/8oz	10 minutes/	20–25 minutes/
	100% (high)	50% (medium)

(See page 16 for instructions on soaking dried beans.)

Rice

LONG-GRAIN WHITE   Place in a large cooking dish with
boiling water, salt and a knob of butter, if liked. Cover
loosely with a lid or vented cling film and cook for 1st time
and power specified. Reduce power setting and cook for 2nd
time specified, stirring twice. Leave to stand, covered, for 5
minutes before serving. Fluff the rice with a fork to separate
to serve.

Quantity	Water	Salt	1st Time/Power	2nd Time/Power
100g/4oz	300ml/½ pint	½ tsp	3 minutes/ 100% (high)	12 minutes/ 50% (medium)
150g/5oz	350ml/12fl oz	½ tsp	3 minutes/ 100% (high)	12 minutes/ 50% (medium)
175g/6oz	400ml/14fl oz	½ tsp	3 minutes/ 100% (high)	12 minutes/ 50% (medium)
200g/7oz	475ml/16fl oz	¾ tsp	3 minutes/ 100% (high)	12 minutes/ 50% (medium)
225g/8oz	550ml/18fl oz	1 tsp	3 minutes/ 100% (high)	12 minutes/ 50% (medium)
275g/10oz	600ml/1 pint	1 tsp	3 minutes/ 100% (high)	12 minutes/ 50% (medium)

LONG-GRAIN BROWN   Place in a large cooking dish with
boiling water, salt and a knob of butter, if liked. Cover
loosely with a lid or vented cling film and cook for 1st time
and power specified. Reduce power setting and cook for 2nd
time specified, stirring 2–3 times. Leave to stand, covered,
for 5 minutes before serving. Fluff the rice with a fork to
separate to serve.

Quantity	Water	Salt	1st Time/Power	2nd Time/Power
100g/4oz	300ml/½ pint	½ tsp	3 minutes/ 100% (high)	25 minutes/ 50% (medium)
150g/5oz	350ml/12fl oz	½ tsp	3 minutes/ 100% (high)	25 minutes/ 50% (medium)
175g/6oz	400ml/14fl oz	½ tsp	3 minutes/ 100% (high)	25 minutes/ 50% (medium)
200g/7oz	475ml/16fl oz	¾ tsp	3 minutes/ 100% (high)	25 minutes/ 50% (medium)

225g/8oz	550ml/18fl oz	1 tsp	3 minutes/ 100% (high)	25 minutes/ 50% (medium)
275g/10oz	600ml/1 pint	1 tsp	3 minutes/ 100% (high)	25 minutes/ 50% (medium)

LONG-GRAIN AND WILD RICE MIX   Place in a large cooking dish with boiling water, salt and a knob of butter. Cover loosely with a lid or vented cling film and cook for 1st time and power specified. Reduce power setting and cook for 2nd time specified, stirring twice. Leave to stand, covered, for 5 minutes before serving. Fluff the rice mixture with a fork to separate to serve.

Quantity mix	Water	Salt	1st Time/Power	2nd Time/Power
1 × 400g/ 14oz packet	700ml/24fl oz	1 tsp	3 minutes/ 100% (high)	12 minutes/ 50% (medium)

FROZEN COOKED RICE   To thaw and reheat, place in a dish, cover and cook for the time specified, stirring twice. Leave to stand, covered, for 2 minutes before using.

Quantity	Power	Minutes
225g/8oz	100% (high)	5–6
450g/1lb	100% (high)	7–8

Also see WILD RICE (page 30).

Rice Pudding

TO COOK ROUND-GRAIN RICE PUDDING   Pour milk and evaporated milk into a large bowl. Add the rice, sugar and a pinch of spice if liked. Cover and cook for 1st time and power specified, stirring 2–3 times. Reduce the power setting and cook for the 2nd time specified, stirring twice. Leave to stand, covered, for 5 minutes before serving.

Milk	Evaporated milk	Rice	Sugar	1st Time/Power	2nd Time/Power
250ml/ 8fl oz	1 × 170g/ 6oz can	5 tbsp	2 tbsp	6–8 minutes/ 100% (high)	30 minutes/ 50% (medium)

TO COOK FLAKED RICE PUDDING Pour milk into a large bowl and cook for 1st time and power specified. Add the rice, sugar, a knob of butter and a pinch of spice if liked. Cover and cook for 2nd time and power specified, stirring once. Leave to stand, covered, for 5 minutes before serving.

Milk	1st Time/Power	Rice	Sugar	2nd Time/Power
600ml/1 pint	6 minutes/ 100% (high)	5 tbsp	2 tbsp	15 minutes/ 50% (medium)

Rose Cocoa or Borlotti Beans (dried)

TO COOK SOAKED BEANS Place soaked beans in a cooking dish. Cover with boiling water. Cover and cook for the 1st time and power specified. Reduce the power setting and cook for the 2nd time specified, adding extra boiling water to cover if needed. Drain to use as required.

Quantity soaked beans	1st Time/Power	2nd Time/Power
225g/8oz	10 minutes/ 100% (high)	20–25 minutes/ 50% (medium)

(See page 16 for instructions on soaking dried beans.)

Rye

RYE GRAINS Soak overnight or for 6–8 hours. Place in a large cooking dish with boiling water and salt. Cover loosely with a lid or vented cling film and cook for 1st time and power specified. Reduce power setting and cook for 2nd time specified, stirring 3 times. Leave to stand, covered, for 5–10 minutes before serving. Fluff the grains with a fork to separate to serve.

Quantity	Water	Salt	1st Time/Power	2nd Time/Power
175g/6oz	750ml/1¼ pints	1 tsp	3 minutes/ 100% (high)	40 minutes/ 50% (medium)

S

Semolina Pudding

TO COOK Place custard powder, semolina, sugar, egg yolks and milk in a dish, mixing well. Cook for 1st time and power specified, stirring twice. Reduce power setting to 30% (low) and cook for 2nd time specified, stirring twice. Fold in 2 stiffly beaten egg whites to serve.

Custard powder	Semolina	Sugar	Egg yolks	Milk	1st Time/Power	2nd Time/Power
4 tsp	25g/1oz	50g/2oz	2	600ml/ 1 pint	8 minutes/ 100% (high)	10 minutes/ 30% (low)

Soya Beans

TO COOK SOAKED BEANS Place soaked beans in a cooking dish. Cover with boiling water. Cover and cook for the 1st time and power specified. Reduce the power setting and cook for the 2nd time specified, adding extra boiling water to cover if needed. Drain to use as required.

Quantity soaked beans	1st Time/Power	2nd Time/Power
225g/8oz	10 minutes/ 100% (high)	20–25 minutes/ 50% (medium)

(See page 16 for instructions on soaking dried beans.)

Split Peas (green and yellow)

TO COOK SOAKED SPLIT PEAS Place soaked split peas in a cooking dish. Cover with boiling water. Cover and cook for the time specified.

Quantity soaked split peas	Power	Minutes
225g/8oz	100% (high)	10

(See page 16 for instructions on soaking dried beans.)

Stock

TO MAKE VEGETABLE STOCK   Place chopped vegetables and peelings in a bowl with the boiling water, a bouquet garni and salt and pepper to taste. Cover and cook for the 1st time and power specified. Reduce the power and cook for the 2nd time specified. Strain and use or cool completely. Store in the refrigerator for up to 24 hours, or freeze for up to 3 months.

Quantity vegetables	Water	1st Time/Power	2nd Time/Power
350g/12oz	1 litre/1¾ pints	10 minutes/ 100% (high)	10–15 minutes/ 50% (medium)

W

Wheat

WHEAT GRAINS   Soak overnight or for 6–8 hours. Place in a large cooking dish with boiling water and salt. Cover loosely with a lid or vented cling film and cook for 1st time and power specified. Reduce power setting and cook for 2nd time specified, stirring 3 times. Leave to stand, covered, for 5–10 minutes before serving. Fluff the wheat grains with a fork to separate to serve.

Quantity	Water	Salt	1st Time/Power	2nd Time/Power
175g/6oz	1 litre/1¾ pints	1 tsp	3 minutes/ 100% (high)	40 minutes/ 50% (medium)

Also see BULGHUR (Cracked Wheat), page 13.

Wild Rice

Soak the rice in 600ml/1 pint warm water for 2–3 hours. Drain thoroughly. Place in a bowl with the oil, boiling water and seasonings to taste. Cover and cook for the time specified, stirring once. Leave to stand, covered, for 5 minutes before serving.

Quantity	Oil	Water	Power	Minutes
100g/4oz	1 tbsp	600ml/1 pint	100% (high)	30

Y

Yogurt

TO MAKE FRESH   Place the milk in a large jug and cook, uncovered, for the time specified (or until boiling). Cover and allow to cool until tepid – up to 30 minutes. Add the live natural yogurt, blending well, and pour into a warmed wide-necked flask. Seal and leave, undisturbed, to set – at least 8 hours.

Quantity milk	Power	Minutes	Live natural yogurt
600ml/1 pint	100% (high)	5–6	3 tbsp

FROZEN   To thaw, remove lid and cook for the time specified. Stir well and leave to stand for 1–2 minutes before serving.

Quantity	Power	Minutes
1 × 142g/5oz carton	100% (high)	1

Vegetarian Nutrition
and Healthy Eating

A vegetarian style of cooking and eating is a nutritious healthy way of living without the need for animal meat, fish, poultry and game. And it is a style of living that is gaining ground year by year. Vegetarians are acquiring a new found credence and respect in the population as a whole and even polled meat-eaters are stating that they are moving nearer to a non-meat eating pattern of feeding, especially cutting down or cutting out red meats.

Many vegetarians choose not to eat meat for many social, compassionate and economic reasons – many more will also quote health grounds for this way of life. The distinction between a healthy vegan, vegetarian and meat-eating diet however has little impact unless a diet is balanced for good health. All food eating groups need to achieve balance between the various nutrients in their diet for healthy living.

The simplest way to promote healthy eating is to ensure a good variety of foods are consumed with all their inherent varied food nutrients. For a diet to be balanced and varied it must supply the right amounts of proteins, fats, carbohydrates, minerals, vitamins and fibre. Eating varied meals and foods is the easiest way to achieve this overall balance.

Vegetarians, by virtue of abstaining from eating certain foods, therefore have to work harder at providing all the essential nutrients for good health. Proteins are often considered the major food group to check on – although vegetarians can find ample protein in eggs, vegetables, milk, cheese, grains, pulses, nuts and seeds. Vegans will find it much tougher with their strict rules on no dairy produce and honey. The bonus is that they are unlikely to suffer from a lack of vitamins and minerals found in such rich quantities in fruit, grains, nuts, seeds and vegetables. For the same reasons they are also unlikely to suffer from lack of fibre and its associated problems. Adequate amounts of fats and carbohydrates are also expected to be found since they go hand in glove with those foods a vegetarian naturally turns to when foregoing meat, fish and poultry.

In essence this should all add up to a varied non-meat eating diet – in theory yes, but in practice perhaps not. Many vegetarians still eat a good quantity (more than advised?) of processed, sweet-toothed, refined products including white sugar, white flour, polished white rice, additive-laden foods and high-salt added products. They too could improve their diets by following the recommendations of the COMA (Committee on Medical Aspects of Food Policy) and NACNE (National Advisory Committee on Nutrition Education) advisors by reducing their overall total fat intake; reducing sugar and refined carbohydrate levels; reducing the consumption of salt; increasing their dietary fibre intake; taking regular daily exercise; reducing consumption of alcohol; and cutting down or cutting out cigarette smoking like the rest of the general population at large. The recipes in this book have tried to implement some of these guidelines without being too bland, boring and strict beyond endurance. Variety is the spice of life and it is often said that the little indulgences in life are the ones that make it worth living, so some recipes do bypass this general theme.

Menu Planning

If you are a novice vegetarian cook then take heart from looking at the many millions of established vegetarians who eat constantly varied meals from day to day, week to week and month to month throughout the year. They do not find it difficult to balance dishes and menus with variety and express surprise when told about the complexity of planning meat-free menus. Certainly familiarity of dishes and their make-up is a great help when planning meals but the old principles of ensuring variety of texture, flavour, colour and weightiness of dishes still rule the day.

The best start is to choose your main course dish – a pasta lasagne, rice or grain pilaff, a vegetarian curry or vegetable nut roast for example. Build around it a selection of light and tasty accompaniments – a vegetable medley, tossed salad selection, grain mixture or selection of bread rolls or crisp crackers. Those decided upon, choose a light or hearty starter which will stimulate the tastebuds. A pudding or dessert is often an easy choice but remember to ring the changes of texture, flavour and colour. If time is at a premium then choose a store cupboard or freezer-proof dish to save time. If there is still room for more then opt for a dairy platter of special cheeses, fresh fruit and nuts or perhaps a slice of home-made teabread, cake or scone.

Trial and error will often tell you where you are going wrong and where you score your best successes – you will quickly build up a repertoire of family favourites. Here are a few ideas for some menus that can be built around the recipes in this book for balanced complete meals:

Suggested Menus

Family Dinner

Edam Corn Chowder   (page 55)
Wholewheat Bread (page 151)
Bean and Aubergine Bake (page 73)
Mixed Green Salad
Lemon Baked Apples (page 145)
  or Cider Poached Pears (page 149)

Special Occasion Dinner

Vegetarian Layered Terrine (page 57)
  or Mushrooms and Peppers à la Grecque (page 164)
Mama Mia's Italian Aubergine and Pasta Mould (page 173)
Mangetout and Salad Greenery in Buttery Avocado Dressing
  (page 109)
Truffled Coconut and Mango Chocolate Loaf (page 181)
  or Yogurt Tangs with Orange Peppercorn Sauce (page 177)
Cheese and Crackers

Summer Informal Lunch Menu

Butter Bean and Sesame Pâté (page 56)
Cream Cheese and Broccoli Quiche (page 61)
Salad Primavera (page 114)
  or Piquant Wholewheat Pasta Salad (page 110)
Pink Summer Salad (page 115)
Redcurrant and Raspberry Yogurt Ice (page 179)
  or Grapefruit, Fromage Frais and Ginger Wedges (page 176)

Winter Lunch Menu

Devilled Mushrooms (page 58)
  or Woodcutter Soup (page 55)
Artichoke and Mozzarella Pizza (page 72)
  or Egg, Fruit and Vegetable Biriyani (page 88)
Cheesy Waldorf Salad (page 112) or Mixed Salad
Tropical Crunch Crumble (page 148)
  or Orange Crème Brulées (page 142)

Buffet Supper Menu

Creamy Mushroom Spread or Dip (page 59)
Oat-Topped Soda Bread (page 152)
Feta and Raisin Stuffed Jackets (page 63)
  or Leek, Horseradish and Cheese Filled Potatoes (page 104)
Wholewheat Macaroni and Mushroom Supper (page 62)
  or Savoury Avocado and Walnut Risotto (page 79)
Mixed Green Salad
Cheesy Apricot and Raspberry Roulade (page 160)

Picnic Menu

Guacamole Pitta Pockets (page 66)
Cheesy Cauliflower in an Onion Crust (page 87)
Fresno Chick Pea and Bean Salad (page 95)
Concertina Salad (page 111)
Mini Pineapple Cheesecakes (page 141)
  or Blackberry Fool (page 139)
Lucy's Flapjacks (page 161)
  or One Cup Cookies (page 161)

Children's Party Menu

Creamy Mushroom Spread (page 59)
Oat-Topped Soda Bread (page 152)
Mini Mozzarella Pizzas (page 67)
Cauliflower and Tomato Cheese (page 60)
  or Double Cheese and Mushroom Spaghetti (page 85)
Cinnamon, Pear and Tofu Flan (page 146)
High Tea Chocolate Loaf (page 156)
  or Crunchy Nut Gingerbread (page 158)

Christmas Dinner Menu

Woodcutter Soup (page 55)
  or Baked Quails' Eggs (page 165)
Mama Mia's Italian Aubergine and Pasta Mould (page 173)
  or Vegetable and Nut Roast (page 77)
Orange-Scented Mushroom and Almond Risotto (page 70)
  or Bulghur and Lentil Pilau (page 94)
Mangetout and Salad Greenery in Buttery Avocado
  Dressing (page 109)
Citrus Orange Charlotte (page 140)
  or Liqueur-Soaked Muesli Trifle (page 182)

Before You Start . . .
Recipe Guidelines

- All the recipes and timings in this book have been tested using ovens with a maximum output of 650–700 watts. The ovens also had variable power and the descriptions used refer to the following power outputs:

100% (High) = 650–700 watts
70% (Medium/High) = 500–550 watts
50% (Medium) = 300–350 watts
30% (Low) = 200 watts
20% (Defrost) = 150 watts

The chart on page 40 gives approximate power outputs in watts at these levels and their relative cooking times; while the chart on page 41 gives adjustment times for ovens of varying maximum output:

How to Use the Cooking Charts

For example: If one of the recipes states 8 minutes at 50% (medium) and your microwave oven has a calibration of 40% (not 50%) then you must look at the figure in the relevant column (40%) which is 10 minutes (and not 8 minutes).

However, if your oven is a 600 watt output model, with a calibration of 40% (not 50%), then as well as the calculated 10 minutes (see above adjustment) you will need to refer to the second chart and add on the relevant 10 seconds per minute, which gives 10 × 10 = 100 seconds extra (approximately 1¾ minutes). So total cooking time will be 10+1¾ minutes = 11¾ minutes.

- The microwave ovens used for testing also had a turntable facility. If yours does not, then follow the basic rules in your microwave handbook for turning, rearranging and rotating foods at regular intervals during the cooking times.
- Metric measurements may vary from one recipe to another within the book for the best results. It is essential to follow either metric or Imperial.
- Note that unless otherwise stated, flour is of the plain variety; water is cold; eggs are size 3; sugar is granulated and all spoon quantities are measured level.
- When dishes are to be covered use either a well-fitting lid, a plate or saucer, greaseproof paper or cling film for this purpose – pure cling is a cling film without added plasticizers and is ideal for lengthy and high temperature cooking.
- It is often difficult to check whether a cheese is suitable for strict vegetarian eating i.e. has been made without the addition of animal rennet. Many vegetarians do not make the distinction and indeed I have not in many of the recipes in this book. However, for information, the following cheeses are principally made without animal rennet but always ask for assurance from your dairy supplier if in doubt: Cheddar, chèvre, cottage, cream, curd, Double Gloucester, feta, Gouda, goat's, munster, ricotta and vegetarian hard.
- Powdered gelatine has been used in some recipes which is animal derived – agar-agar may be substituted in powdered form but packet instructions should always be followed for preparation (usually the agar-agar is added to cold liquid and then boiled in order to set). Use approximately 2 level tsp of powdered agar-agar to set 600ml (1 pint) of liquid. Measure the total liquids in the recipe, add the agar-agar to some of it and boil, then add the remainder quickly and blend well. Use quickly since the mixture sets with speed and does not require chilling to set. Unlike powdered gelatine which comes in 11g/0.4oz packets, agar-agar comes in sachets containing almost 4 tbsp of powder.
- Ideally use home-made vegetable stock for the best flavour and results – when time is short use vegetable stock cubes.
- When ghee has been used it should be of the vegetable type.
- Government guidelines now recommend that cling film with plasticizers, i.e. pvc film, should not be used as a covering or lining for foods cooked in the microwave. All cling film referred to in this book is of the 'polyethylene' film type without

plasticizers and can be found under such brand names as Purecling, Saran Wrap and Glad Wrap. This type of film does not cling as well as standard pvc film but can often be more manageable when pulling back to stir food during cooking. If you do not wish to use cling film as a covering then use an upturned plate, saucer, special microwave plate cover or baking parchment instead.

1 Guide to comparative microwave oven control settings

	20% (defrost)	30% (low)		50% (medium)		70% (medium/high)	100% (high)
Descriptions of settings used in this book	1	2	3	4	5	6	7
Descriptions of settings available on popular microwave ovens	keep warm / low / 2	simmer / 3	stew / medium/low / 4	defrost / medium / 5	bake / medium / 6	roast / high / 7–8	full/high / normal / 10
Approximate % power input	20%	30%	40%	50%	60%	70%	100%
Approximate power output in watts	150W	200W	250W	300–350W	400W	500–550W	650–700W
Cooking time in minutes (for times greater than 10 minutes simply add the figures in the appropriate columns)	4	3¼	2½	2	1¾	1¼	1
	8	6¾	5	4	3¼	2¾	2
	12	10	7½	6	5	4	3
	16	13¼	10	8	6¾	5¼	4
	20	16¾	12½	10	8¼	6¾	5
	24	20	15	12	10	8	6
	28	23¼	17½	14	12	9¼	7
	32	26¾	20	16	13¼	10¾	8
	36	30	22½	18	15	12	9
	40	33¾	25	20	16½	13¼	10

2 Cooking times adjustment chart

For each minute of cooking time at 650–700 watts (high) in the recipes:

Add 10 seconds at 600 watts per minute of cooking time

Add 25 seconds at 500 watts per minute of cooking time

Add 45 seconds at 400 watts per minute of cooking time

(For example: 6 minutes on 100% (high) at 650–700 watts would be adjusted to +45 × 6 for a 400 watt oven (i.e. 270 seconds or 4½ minutes) therefore cooking time would be advised to + 4½ = 10½ minutes for a 400 watt oven.

Recipes

Better Breakfasts
and Brunches

Creamy Raisin Porridge

Serves: 4
Power setting: 30% (low)
Total cooking time: 6–7 minutes

300ml/½ pint milk
600ml/1 pint water
pinch of ground cinnamon
75g/3oz quick-cook porridge oats
50g/2oz raisins
low-fat yogurt to serve

Place the milk, water, cinnamon, oats and raisins in a large bowl, blending well. Cover with vented cling film and microwave at 30% (low) for 6–7 minutes, stirring twice. Leave to stand, covered, for 3 minutes.

Stir well and spoon into individual serving bowls. Top with a swirl of yogurt and serve at once.

Crunchy Muesli

Serves: 8–10
Power setting: 100% (high)
Total cooking time: 4–6 minutes

350g/12oz oats
100g/4oz flaked coconut
75g/3oz hazelnuts
75g/3oz sesame seeds
50g/2oz wheatgerm
100ml/4fl oz clear honey
50ml/2fl oz sunflower oil
175g/6oz raisins

Preheat a large browning dish according to the manufacturer's instructions, about 6 minutes at 100% (high).

Meanwhile, mix the oats with the coconut, hazelnuts, sesame seeds, wheatgerm, honey and oil, blending well.

Add to the browning dish and stir quickly on all sides to crispen and lightly brown. Microwave at 100% (high) for 4–6 minutes, stirring every 1 minute.

Stir in the raisins and allow to cool. Transfer to an airtight container to store.

Serve with milk, yogurt or fruit juice as liked.

Raisin Breakfast Scones

Makes: 12–14
Power setting: 100% (high)
Total cooking time: 7–9 minutes

225g/8oz self-raising wholemeal flour
2 tsp baking powder
pinch of salt
50g/2oz raisins
25g/1oz light brown sugar
1 egg
300ml/½ pint milk
vegetable oil

Sift the flour, baking powder and salt into a bowl. Stir in the raisins and sugar, blending well. Make a well in the centre of the dry ingredients and add the egg. Gradually beat in the milk, a little at a time, blending well to make a smooth batter.

Preheat a large browning dish according to the manufacturer's instructions, about 6 minutes at 100% (high). Brush lightly with a little oil and microwave at 100% (high) for a further ½ minute. Place about 4 heaped tablespoons of the batter on to the dish, a little apart and microwave at 100% (high) for 1 minute or until the mixture bubbles on the surface. Turn over with a spatula and press down well. Microwave at 100% (high) for ½ minute until cooked. Keep warm in a tea towel while cooking the remaining mixture in batches of 4 scones at a time, preheating the browning dish at 100% (high) for 1–2 minutes between cooking the batches.

Serve warm, lightly buttered.

Cranberry and Raisin Muffins

Makes: 18
Power setting: 100% (high)
Total cooking time: 6–9 minutes

4 tbsp sunflower oil
75g/3oz soft dark brown sugar
75g/3oz honey
2 eggs, beaten
250ml/8fl oz milk
50g/2oz bran
75g/3oz raisins
100g/4oz cranberry sauce
150g/5oz self-raising wholemeal flour
1 tsp baking powder
½ tsp bicarbonate of soda
½ tsp salt

Beat the oil with the sugar, honey, eggs and milk. Add the bran, raisins and cranberry sauce, blending well. Sift the flour with the baking powder, bicarbonate of soda and salt and stir into the cranberry mixture, mixing lightly.

Line a microwave muffin pan or 6 small teacups with double-thickness paper bun cases. Fill each two thirds full with the mixture. Microwave at 100% (high) for 2–3 minutes, until cooked and firm to the touch, giving the pan a half-turn once or rearranging the cups once. Remove from the pan, peel away one of the cases to serve. Repeat twice with the remaining mixture to make a total of 18 muffins.

Serve warm, split and buttered.

Wheatgerm and Peach Porridge Steamers

Serves: 4
Power setting: 30% (low)
Total cooking time: 6–7 minutes

300ml/½ pint milk
600ml/1 pint water
75g/3oz quick cook porridge oats

75g/3oz chopped no-need-to-soak dried peaches or apricots
4–6 tsp toasted wheatgerm
milk or yogurt to serve

Place the milk, water, oats and peaches (or apricots) in a
large bowl, blending well. Cover with vented cling film and
microwave at 30% (low) for 6–7 minutes, stirring twice.
Leave to stand, covered, for 3 minutes.

Stir well and spoon into individual serving bowls. Sprinkle
with the toasted wheatgerm. Serve at once with milk or
yogurt.

Cheesy Spinach and Egg Ramekins

Serves: 4
Power setting: 100% (high) and 50% (medium)
Total cooking time: 15–18 minutes

450g/1lb spinach leaves, trimmed and washed
50g/2oz soft cheese with herbs and garlic
90ml/6 tbsp soured cream
salt and pepper
pinch of ground nutmeg or mace
4 eggs
50g/2oz grated cheese
toast fingers to serve

Place the spinach in a bowl without any additional water.
Cover and microwave at 100% (high) for 6–8 minutes,
stirring once. Drain well then press through a nylon sieve
to extract as much juice as possible. Add the soft cheese,
half of the soured cream, salt and pepper to taste and the
nutmeg, blending well. Divide equally between four large
ramekins or heatproof dishes and make a hollow in the
centre of each.

Carefully crack an egg into each spinach hollow and prick
the yolks with the tip of a knife. Spoon over the remaining
soured cream. Sprinkle equally with the grated cheese and
cover loosely with cling film. Microwave at 50% (medium)
for 7–9 minutes or until the eggs are just set and the cheese
has melted.

Serve at once with warm toast fingers.

NOTE: This recipe can be made using a 275g/10oz packet frozen chopped spinach. Place in a bowl, cover and microwave at 100% (high) for 7–9 minutes, stirring to break up twice. Drain and press through a sieve to remove excess juice and continue as above.

Rosé Brunch

Serves: 4
Power setting: 50% (medium)
Total cooking time: ¼–½ minute

2 rosé or pink grapefruit
2 oranges
25g/1oz butter or margarine
8 slices rye or pumperknickel bread
lettuce leaves
¼ cucumber, sliced
50g/2oz cream cheese
50g/2oz fromage frais
1 tbsp snipped chives
salt and pepper

Remove a little zest from the grapefruit and oranges and cut into thin julienne strips to make about 1 tablespoon. Remove the remaining peel, pith and pips and cut the fruit into segments.

Lightly butter the bread and place two slices overlapping slightly on to each individual serving plate. Top with lettuce leaves and cucumber slices.

Arrange the fruit segments on top of the bread alternating the fruit type to make a half circle.

Place the cream cheese in a bowl and microwave at 50% (medium) for ¼–½ minute to soften. Add the fromage frais and beat well to blend. Add the chives and salt and pepper to taste and spoon evenly into the centre of the bread. Garnish with the prepared fruit zest. Serve as soon as possible.

Sunday Brunch Triangles

Serves: 2
Power setting: 100% (high)
Total cooking time: 3–4¼ minutes

100g/4oz mushrooms, wiped and halved or thickly sliced
15g/½oz butter or margarine
2 tomatoes, sliced
3 slices wholemeal toast
3 slices quick-melting cheese

Place the mushrooms in a bowl with the butter. Cover and microwave at 100% (high) for 2–3 minutes, until cooked, stirring once. Drain thoroughly.

Arrange the tomatoes evenly on the toasted bread. Top with the mushrooms then cover with the cheese slices. Place on a double sheet of absorbent kitchen towel, without overlapping and microwave at 100% (high) for 1–1¼ minutes or until the cheese melts.

Cut the slices of bread into triangles and serve at once.

Cinnamon French Toasts

Serves: 2–4
Power setting: 100% (high)
Total cooking time: 3–3½ minutes

2 eggs, beaten
2 tbsp milk
¼ tsp ground cinnamon
1 tsp brown sugar
40g/1½oz butter or margarine
4 thick slices bread

Preheat a large browning dish according to the manufacturer's instructions, about 6 minutes at 100% (high).

Meanwhile beat the eggs with the milk, cinnamon and sugar in a large shallow dish. Add the butter to the browning dish and swirl quickly over the base to melt. Dip the bread into the egg mixture and press down on to the browning dish. Microwave at 100% (high) for 1–1½ minutes, turn over and rearrange then microwave at 100% (high) for a further 2 minutes.

Serve at once cut into triangles with syrup, honey or extra butter.

Spiced Fruity Breakfast Cup

Serves: 4
Power setting: 100% (high)
Total cooking time: 4–5 minutes

300ml/½ pint water
100g/4oz demerara sugar
3 tbsp lemon juice
pinch of ground nutmeg
pinch of ground cloves
pinch of ground cinnamon
2 allspice berries
½ cantaloupe or ogen melon, peeled, seeded and scooped into balls
2 ruby or pink grapefruit, peeled, pith removed and segmented
1 ripe peach or nectarine, stoned and sliced
1 banana, peeled and sliced
1 green dessert apple, cored and sliced
2 fresh figs, peeled and quartered (optional)

Place the water, sugar, lemon juice and spices in a bowl. Microwave at 100% (high) for 4–5 minutes or until boiling, stirring every 1 minute to ensure that the sugar dissolves.

Add the fruit and stir well to coat and blend in the spiced syrup. Cover and leave to stand for 5 minutes before serving.

Serve warm, plain or topped with a little soured cream or thick set natural yogurt.

Melon Balls in Minted Syrup

Serves: 4
Power setting: 100% (high)
Total cooking time: 10 minutes

75g/3oz castor sugar
300ml/½ pint water
handful of mint, chopped
juice of 1 lemon
1 large honeydew melon or mixture of charentais, ogen, water and
  honeydew melon

Place the sugar and water in a large bowl. Microwave at
100% (high) for 10 minutes, stirring 3 times to ensure the
sugar has dissolved and the syrup is boiling and thickened.
Add the lemon juice and mint and leave to cool.

When cool place the syrup in a blender and purée until
the mint leaves are very finely chopped.

Scoop the melon flesh into balls using a melon baller or
teaspoon and place in a serving bowl. Pour the syrup over
and mix well to coat. Cover and chill thoroughly before
serving.

Starters, Light Lunches and Snacks

Woodcutter Soup

Serves: 4
Power setting: 100% (high)
Total cooking time: 9 minutes

50g/2oz butter or margarine
40g/1½oz plain flour
600ml/1 pint hot vegetable stock
450ml/¾ pint milk
225g/8oz button mushrooms, wiped and sliced
4 tbsp chopped watercress
50g/2oz pine nuts
salt and pepper

Place the butter or margarine in a bowl and microwave at 100% (high) for 1 minute to melt. Add the flour, blending well. Gradually add the hot vegetable stock, milk, mushrooms and watercress, blending well. Cover and microwave at 100% (high) for 6 minutes, stirring briskly every 2 minutes.

Add the pine nuts and salt and pepper to taste. Cover and microwave at 100% (high) for 2 minutes until hot and the flavours are well blended.

Serve hot with granary bread rolls.

Edam Corn Chowder

Serves: 4
Power setting: 100% (high)
Total cooking time: 5–7 minutes

340g/12oz can sweetcorn kernels
150ml/¼ pint natural yogurt
½ tsp curry powder
1 vegetable stock cube
1 tsp cornflour
150ml/¼ pint hot water
salt and pepper
75g/3oz Edam cheese, grated
snipped chives to garnish

Place three-quarters of the sweetcorn in a blender with all of the corn juice from the can. Add the yogurt, curry powder, stock cube, cornflour, water and salt and pepper to taste. Purée until smooth then pour into a bowl.

Microwave at 100% (high) for 4–5 minutes or until hot and creamy but not boiling. Stir in 50g/2oz of the cheese, blending well. Microwave at 100% (high) for 1–2 minutes to reheat then pour into 4 individual serving bowls.

Serve sprinkled with the remaining cheese and garnished with snipped chives. Serve at once.

Butter Bean and Sesame Paté

Serves: 4
Power setting: 100% (high)
Total cooking time: 4 minutes

1 onion, peeled and finely chopped
1 garlic clove, peeled and crushed
4 tsp olive oil
450g/15oz can butter beans, drained
1 tbsp cream
1 tbsp toasted sesame seeds
½ tsp wholegrain mustard
½ tsp wine vinegar
salt and pepper
4 spring onions, trimmed and very finely chopped

Place the onion, garlic and oil in a bowl. Cover and microwave at 100% (high) for 4 minutes, stirring once. Place in a blender with the butter beans, cream and half of the sesame seeds and purée until chunky.

Add the mustard, wine vinegar, salt and pepper to taste and the spring onions, mixing well to blend. Spoon into one large or four small individual serving dishes.

Sprinkle with the remaining sesame seeds and serve lightly chilled with rye crackers or Melba toast.

Vegetarian Layered Terrine

Serves: 6–8
Power setting: 100% (high)
Total cooking time: 4½–5½ minutes

4 hard-boiled eggs, shelled and chopped
300ml/½ pint mayonnaise
150ml/¼ pint quark
150ml/¼ pint soured cream
¼ onion, peeled and grated
salt and pepper
225g/8oz broccoli spears
6 tbsp cold water
85g/3oz packet soft cheese with garlic and herbs
1 tbsp chopped parsley
5 tsp powdered gelatine or 25g/1oz agar-agar
100ml/4oz boiling water
3 tbsp lemon juice

Mix the hard-boiled eggs with half of the mayonnaise, half of the quark, half of the soured cream, the onion and salt and pepper to taste, blending well.

Place the broccoli in a bowl with 4 tablespoons of the cold water. Cover and microwave at 100% (high) for 4–5 minutes until tender, rearranging once. Carefully trim away about half of the broccoli spear heads and reserve for the garnish. Place the remaining broccoli in a blender with the remaining mayonnaise, quark, soured cream, soft cheese, parsley and salt and pepper to taste. Purée until smooth.

Dissolve all but 1 teaspoon of the gelatine in the boiling water (if using agar-agar then follow the packet instructions using cold water and bring to the boil). Stir half into the egg mixture and half into the broccoli mixture, blending well.

Spoon half of the egg mixture into the base of a 1.2 litre/ 2 pint loaf dish or terrine and chill to set. Cover with half of the broccoli mixture and chill to set. Repeat the egg and broccoli layers once more, chilling and setting between each.

Place the remaining gelatine in a bowl with the lemon

juice and microwave at 100% (high) for ½ minute to dissolve (if using agar-agar follow the packet instructions using the lemon juice). Add the remaining cold water and blend well. Arrange the reserved broccoli heads on top of the terrine, cut into halves if large and then position cut sides up and spoon over the lemon glaze to coat. Chill thoroughly.

Serve cut into thin slices with toasted or hot French bread.

Devilled Mushrooms

Serves: 4
Power setting: 100% (high)
Total cooking time: 5–6 minutes

24 cup mushrooms, wiped
25g/1oz butter or margarine
1 tbsp lemon juice
Devilled Sauce:
150ml/¼ pint double cream
1 tbsp tomato purée
2 tsp horseradish relish
1 tbsp malt vinegar
2 tsp Worcestershire sauce
½ tsp French mustard
salt and pepper

Trim the stalks of the mushrooms level with the cups. Place the butter in a bowl and microwave at 100% (high) for 1 minute to melt. Add the lemon juice and mushrooms and microwave at 100% (high) for 1 minute, stirring once. Place in a serving dish with the stalks uppermost.

Whip the cream until it stands in soft peaks. Fold in the tomato purée, horseradish relish, malt vinegar, Worcestershire sauce, French mustard and salt and pepper to taste, blending well. Spread over the mushrooms and microwave at 100% (high) for 3–4 minutes, until the mushrooms are cooked and tender.

Serve hot on lightly buttered toast or over boiled rice.

Creamy Mushroom Spread or Dip

Serves: 4–6
Power setting: 100% (high)
Total cooking time: 4 minutes

225g/8oz cup mushrooms, wiped
100g/4oz butter or margarine
1 tbsp grated onion
85g/3oz packet full-fat cream cheese
few drops Worcestershire sauce
salt and pepper
lemon juice
parsley sprigs to garnish

Place the mushrooms in a bowl with the butter and onion. Cover and microwave at 100% (high) for 4 minutes, stirring once.

Place in a blender or liquidizer with the cheese, Worcestershire sauce and salt and pepper to taste. Purée until well blended then pour into one large or 4–6 small ramekins or dishes and chill to set.

Serve lightly chilled garnished with parsley sprigs. Serve with wholemeal toast or as a dip for crisp vegetable sticks.

Tagliatelle with Bolina Sauce

Serves: 4
Power setting: 100% (high) and 50% (medium)
Total cooking time: 9½–10½ minutes

275g/10oz dried tagliatelle
1.5 litres/2½ pints boiling water
1 tsp oil
125g/4½oz packet Danish Bolina cheese or other rich smooth cheese with blue veining
25g/1oz butter
4 tbsp single cream
2 tbsp chopped fresh parsley
salt and pepper

Place the pasta in a large bowl with the water and oil. Cover loosely and microwave at 100% (high) for 6 minutes, stirring once. Leave to stand for 3–5 minutes then drain thoroughly.

Meanwhile, place the cheese and butter in a bowl and microwave at 50% (medium) for 2–3 minutes, until melted and creamy, stirring twice. Add the cream and parsley and cook at 50% (medium) for a further 1½ minutes, stirring once.

Pour the sauce over the pasta and toss gently to coat. Serve at once with crusty bread and a crisp mixed salad.

Cauliflower and Tomato Cheese

Serves: 2
Power setting: 100% (high)
Total cooking time: 12–13 minutes

½ cauliflower, broken into florets
4 carrots, peeled and cut into julienne strips
4 tbsp water
240g/8oz can tomato sauce
50g/2oz wholemeal breadcrumbs
50g/2oz vegetarian hard cheese, grated
25g/1oz unsalted peanuts, coarsely chopped
parsley sprigs to garnish

Place the cauliflower, carrots and water in a medium baking dish. Cover and microwave at 100% (high) for 8–9 minutes, until tender, stirring once. Drain thoroughly. Mix with the tomato sauce and return to the dish.

Mix the breadcrumbs with the cheese and peanuts and sprinkle over the vegetable mixture. Microwave at 100% (high) for 4 minutes, or until the cheese has melted and the vegetables are tender. Brown under a preheated hot grill if liked.

Serve hot, garnished with parsley sprigs.

Cream Cheese and Broccoli Quiche

Serves: 6
Power setting: 100% (high) and 30% (low)
Total cooking time: 22½–24½ minutes

20cm/8in ready-cooked flan case or 175g/6oz wholewheat pastry
175g/6oz broccoli
2 tbsp water
175g/6oz Boursin with garlic and herbs
3 eggs, beaten
5 tbsp single cream
2 tbsp milk
3 spring onions, trimmed and chopped
salt and pepper
cucumber and tomato slices to garnish

If using pastry, roll out on a lightly floured surface to a round large enough to line the base and sides of a 20cm/8in flan dish. Press in firmly, taking care not to stretch. Cut the pastry away leaving a 5mm/¼in 'collar' above the dish to allow for any shrinkage. Prick the base and sides well with a fork. Place a double thickness layer of absorbent kitchen towel over the base, easing it into position round the edges. Microwave at 100% (high) for 3½ minutes, giving the dish a quarter turn every 1 minute. Remove the paper and microwave at 100% (high) for a further 1½ minutes.

To make the filling, place the broccoli and water in a bowl. Cover and microwave at 100% (high) for 3½ minutes. Drain and chop coarsely. Spread over the base of the cooked flan. Beat the cheese with the eggs, cream, milk, spring onions and salt and pepper to taste. Pour over the broccoli and microwave at 30% (low) for 14–16 minutes, turning the dish every 3 minutes, or until just cooked and set in the centre.

Leave to stand for 10–15 minutes before serving warm or cold garnished with cucumber and tomato slices.

Wholewheat Macaroni and Mushroom Supper

Serves: 4
Power setting: 100% (high)
Total cooking time: 16 minutes

225g/8oz wholewheat macaroni
1.2 litres/2 pints boiling water
2 tbsp vegetable oil
2 large sticks celery, scrubbed and sliced
275g/10oz open mushrooms, wiped and sliced
4 tomatoes, peeled and chopped
1 tsp onion or garlic purée
salt and pepper
100g/4oz Double Gloucester or vegetarian hard cheese, grated
chopped parsley to garnish

Place the macaroni in a large bowl with the boiling water.
Cover loosely and microwave at 100% (high) for 10
minutes, until tender, stirring once. Leave to stand for 3
minutes then drain thoroughly.

Place the oil, celery, mushrooms and onion or garlic purée
in a large bowl. Cover and microwave at 100% (high) for
3 minutes, stirring once.

Add the macaroni, salt and pepper to taste and cheese,
blending well. Spoon into a serving dish and microwave at
100% (high) for 3 minutes or until the cheese melts and the
mixture is thoroughly reheated.

Serve hot, sprinkled with chopped parsley.

Dutch Aubergine Bake

Serves: 4
Power setting: 100% (high)
Total cooking time: 24½–27½ minutes

450g/1lb aubergines, cut into 1cm/½ inch slices
15g/½oz butter or margarine
350g/12oz leeks, trimmed, washed and thinly sliced
225g/8oz Edam cheese
150ml/¼ pint soured cream or natural yogurt

salt and pepper
1 tsp dried oregano

Place the aubergines on a large flat plate or microwave
baking tray. Place the butter or margarine in a bowl and
microwave at 100% (high) for ½ minute to melt. Brush
over the aubergine slices then microwave at 100% (high)
for 6–7 minutes until softened, turning over and rearranging
once.

Place the leeks in a bowl, cover and microwave at 100%
(high) for 5 minutes, stirring once. Grate half of the cheese
and cut the remainder into thin fingers or triangles.

Place half of the aubergine slices in a shallow cooking
dish. Cover with half of the leeks, half of the grated cheese
and the soured cream or yogurt. Season to taste with salt
and pepper. Repeat the aubergine and leek layers then top
with the cheese slices arranged around the edge of the dish.
Sprinkle the centre of the dish with grated cheese and
oregano. Cover and microwave at 100% (high) for 10
minutes, giving the dish a half turn twice. Brown under a
preheated hot grill if liked or leave to stand for 3–5 minutes
before serving with a tomato and onion side salad and
crusty bread.

Feta and Raisin Stuffed Jackets

Serves: 4–8
Power setting: 100% (high)
Total cooking time: 14–17 minutes

4 × 175g/6oz potatoes, scrubbed
100g/4oz feta or vegetarian hard cheese, diced
2 spring onions, trimmed and chopped
50g/2oz raisins
1 tbsp chopped parsley
½ tsp ground paprika
½ tsp mustard powder
2 tbsp natural yogurt
salt and pepper
tomato slices and parsley sprigs to garnish

Prick the potato skins and place on a double sheet of absorbent kitchen towel. Microwave at 100% (high) for 12–15 minutes, turning over once. Leave to stand for 4 minutes then cut in halves and scoop out the cooked flesh into a bowl.

Mash the potato until smooth then add the cheese, spring onions, raisins, parsley, paprika, mustard, yogurt and salt and pepper to taste, blending well.

Pile the filling back into the potato jackets and top each with a slice of tomato. Microwave at 100% (high) for 2 minutes to reheat.

Serve hot, garnished with parsley sprigs.

Broccoli and Mushroom Gratin

Serves: 4
Power setting: 100% (high)
Total cooking time: 21–23 minutes

50g/2oz butter or margarine
2 onions, peeled and finely chopped
1 tsp cumin seeds
40g/1½oz plain flour
300ml/½ pint milk
300ml/½ pint vegetable stock
few drops of Tabasco sauce
1 bay leaf
350g/12oz broccoli, cut into even-sized pieces
100g/4oz mushrooms, wiped and quartered
salt and pepper
2 eggs, soft-boiled
Topping:
25g/1oz wholewheat breadcrumbs
50g/2oz grated Parmesan cheese
2 tbsp chopped parsley

Place the butter or margarine in a bowl and microwave at 100% (high) for ½ minute to melt. Add the onion and cumin seeds, blending well. Cover and microwave at 100% (high) for 3 minutes, stirring once. Stir in the flour and microwave at 100% (high) for ½ minute. Gradually add the milk, stock and Tabasco and microwave at 100% (high) for 7–9 minutes, stirring every 2 minutes until smooth, boiling and thickened.

Add the bay leaf, broccoli, mushrooms and salt and pepper to taste. Cover loosely and microwave at 100% (high) for 8 minutes, stirring twice. Remove the bay leaf and cover and microwave at 100% (high) for a further 6 minutes, or until the vegetables are fork tender. Leave to stand while preparing the topping.

Mix the breadcrumbs with the Parmesan cheese and parsley, blending well. Roughly chop the eggs and stir into the broccoli mixture. Spoon into a shallow cooking dish and sprinkle over the topping. Microwave at 100% (high) for 2 minutes. Brown under a preheated hot grill if liked.

Serve hot with warm crusty wholemeal rolls.

Mexican Bean Crunch

Serves: 4
Power setting: 100% (high)
Total cooking time: 9 minutes

1 tsp vegetable oil
1 onion, peeled and sliced
2 sticks celery, scrubbed and sliced
1 small red pepper, cored, seeded and sliced
225g/8oz can baked beans in tomato sauce
1 tsp hot chilli powder
1 tbsp chopped parsley
salt and pepper
25g/1oz corn chips
50g/2oz vegetarian hard cheese, grated

Place the oil, onion, celery and pepper in a bowl. Cover and microwave at 100% (high) for 5 minutes, stirring once.

Add the beans, chilli powder, parsley, salt and pepper to taste, blending well. Spoon into a shallow serving dish, cover and microwave at 100% (high) for 2 minutes, stirring once.

Sprinkle with the corn chips and cheese and microwave at 100% (high) for 2 minutes or until the cheese is melted. Brown and crisp under a preheated hot grill if liked. Serve hot with a crisp salad.

Guacomole Pitta Pockets

Serves: 4
Power setting: 100% (high)
Total cooking time: 1 minute

4 large round pitta breads
1 ripe avocado, peeled, stoned and chopped
1 garlic clove, peeled and crushed
1 tbsp lemon juice
3 tbsp natural yogurt
2 tbsp cottage cheese
25g/1oz wholemeal breadcrumbs
1 tsp Worcestershire sauce
pinch of chilli seasoning
salt and pepper
2 tomatoes, chopped
¼ cucumber, chopped
213g/7½oz can red kidney beans, drained
shredded lettuce

Place the pitta breads on a large plate. Microwave, uncovered, at 100% (high) for 1 minute, until hot. Fold each pitta bread in half.

Meanwhile, place the avocado, garlic, lemon juice, yogurt and cottage cheese in a blender and purée until smooth. Add the breadcrumbs, Worcestershire sauce, chilli seasoning and salt and pepper to taste, blending well. Fold in the tomato, cucumber and kidney beans, blending well.

Spoon into the pitta halves and serve on a bed of shredded lettuce.

Vegeburger in a Bun

Serves: 1
Power setting: 100% (high) and 70% (medium high)
Total cooking time: 3¼ minutes

2 tsps vegetable oil
2 × 50g/2oz frozen plain or cheese vegeburgers
a little shredded lettuce or Chinese cabbage
1 hamburger or sesame seeded bun, split
1 tomato, sliced
1 slice quick-melting cheese
few slices dill cucumber or gherkin
1 tbsp tomato pickle, ketchup or relish

Preheat a browning dish according to the manufacturer's instructions, about 6 minutes at 100% (high). Brush with the oil, add the vegeburgers, pressing down well and microwave at 100% (high) for 3 minutes turning over once, until cooked.

Cover the base of the bun with lettuce or Chinese cabbage and top with a cooked vegeburger. Cover with the tomato, the remaining vegeburger, cheese, dill pickle or gherkin and tomato pickle, ketchup or relish. Replace the lid of the bun and press down, lightly.

Reheat at 70% (medium high) for 15 seconds to serve.

Mini Mozzarella Pizzas

Serves: 6
Power setting: 100% (high)
Total cooking time: 4–6 minutes

Base:
75g/3oz wheatmeal flour
25g/1oz butter or margarine
75g/3oz muesli
2 tsp baking powder
½ tsp salt
5 tbsp milk

Topping:
3 tomatoes, finely sliced
garlic salt
1 tsp dried Herbes de Provence
50g/2oz mushrooms, wiped and sliced
100g/4oz Mozzarella cheese, sliced
6 black olives

Place the flour in a bowl and rub in the butter or margarine until the mixture resembles fine breadcrumbs. Stir in the muesli, baking powder and salt, blending well. Add the milk and mix to a smooth soft dough. Divide into six portions and roll each out to a 10cm/4in circle. Place in a ring pattern on a large plate or microwave baking tray. Microwave at 100% (high) for 2–3 minutes, turning over once until just cooked.

Top each pizza base with an equal quantity of the tomato slices and season with garlic salt. Sprinkle with the herbs and mushroom slices then top with the cheese slices. Garnish with a black olive and microwave at 100% (high) for 2–3 minutes until the cheese is bubbly. Leave to stand for 3 minutes before serving.

No Meat Main Meals

Orange-Scented Mushroom and Almond Risotto

Serves: 4–6
Power setting: 100% (high) and 50% (medium)
Total cooking time: 30 minutes

1 large onion, peeled and chopped
225g/8oz long-grain brown rice
225g/8oz closed cup mushrooms, wiped and sliced
grated rind of 1 orange
1½ tsp ground mace
2 tsp vegetable stock extract
550ml/18fl oz boiling water
100g/4oz blanched almonds, chopped
100g/4oz raisins
salt and pepper

Place the onion, rice, mushrooms, orange rind and mace in a large bowl. Mix the vegetable stock extract with the boiling water and pour over the rice mixture. Cover loosely with a lid or vented cling film and microwave at 100% (high) for 5 minutes, stirring once. Reduce the power setting to 50% (medium) and microwave for a further 25 minutes, stirring 2–3 times.

Add the almonds, raisins and salt and pepper to taste, blending well. Cover and leave to stand, tightly covered, for 5 minutes. Fluff the rice with a fork to separate before serving.

Savoury Bean Crumble

Serves: 4
Power setting: 100% (high) and 50% (medium)
Total cooking time: 8–9 minutes

1 tsp vegetable oil
1 onion, peeled and sliced
2 sticks celery, scrubbed and sliced
1 small red pepper, cored, seeded and chopped
25g/8oz can curried beans with sultanas
1 tbsp chopped parsley

225g/1oz plain crisps, coarsely crushed
50g/2oz Cheddar or vegetarian hard cheese, grated
15g/½oz butter or margarine

Place the oil, onion, celery and red pepper in a bowl, cover and microwave at 100% (high) for 4 minutes, stirring once. Add the curried beans and parsley, blending well. Microwave at 100% (high) for 2 minutes, stirring once. Spoon into an ovenproof dish.

Mix the crisps with the cheese and sprinkle over the bean mixture. Dot with the butter and microwave at 50% (medium) for 2–3 minutes or until the cheese has melted. Brown under a preheated hot grill if liked.

Serve hot with crusty bread and a crisp seasonal salad.

Mushroom and Nut Pilaff

Serves: 4–6
Power setting: 100% (high) and 50% (medium)
Total cooking time: 38 minutes

2 tbsp vegetable oil
225g/8oz long-grain brown rice
600ml/1 pint boiling water
1 onion, peeled and sliced
1 garlic clove, peeled and crushed
2 sticks celery, scrubbed and chopped
1 red pepper, cored, seeded and chopped
75g/3oz cashew nuts, chopped
225g/8oz closed cup mushrooms, wiped and quartered
½ tsp Tabasco sauce
salt and pepper

Place half of the oil and the rice in a large bowl. Cook, uncovered, at 100% (high) for 1 minute. Add the water, blending well, cover and microwave at 100% (high) for 3 minutes. Reduce the power setting to 50% (medium) and cook for a further 25 minutes, stirring twice, until the rice is tender and all the water has been absorbed.

Place the remaining oil in a bowl with the onion, garlic, celery, peppers, nuts, mushrooms, Tabasco and salt and pepper to taste. Cover tightly and microwave at 100% (high) for 7 minutes, stirring once. Stir into the cooked rice, blending well. Cover and reheat at 100% (high) for 2 minutes.

Serve hot with a crisp green salad.

Artichoke and Mozzarella Pizza

Serves: 4
Power setting: 100% (high)
Total cooking time: 12½–14 minutes

150g/5oz self-raising wholewheat flour
pinch of salt
25g/1oz butter or margarine
1 egg, beaten
1 tbsp milk
Topping:
1 tbsp oil
1 onion, peeled and chopped
1 garlic clove, crushed
50g/2oz mushrooms, chopped
220g/8oz can chopped tomatoes or
2 tomatoes, peeled, seeded and chopped
1 tbsp tomato purée
1 tsp dried rosemary
salt and pepper
4 canned artichoke hearts, halved
100g/4oz mozarella cheese, sliced
black olives (optional)

Mix the flour with the salt. Rub in the butter or margarine until the mixture resembles fine breadcrumbs. Add the egg and milk and mix to a smooth dough. Roll out on a lightly floured surface and use to line the base of an 18cm/7 inch pie plate. Cover with a domed lid or inverted plate covered with greaseproof paper and microwave at 100% (high) for 3½–4 minutes, giving the plate a quarter turn every minute.

Place the oil, onion, garlic and mushrooms in a bowl. Cover and microwave at 100% (high) for 3 minutes, stirring once. Add the tomatoes, tomato purée, rosemary and salt and pepper to taste. Microwave, uncovered, at 100% (high) for 4 minutes, stirring once.

Spoon the topping over the base, top with the artichoke hearts, cheese and olives if used. Microwave at 100% (high) for 2–3 minutes or until the cheese melts and is hot and bubbly.

Serve at once cut into thick wedges with a crisp salad.

Bean and Aubergine Bake

Serves: 6
Power setting: 100% (high)
Total cooking time: 25–27 minutes

1 onion, peeled and chopped
1 carrot, peeled and chopped
1 stick celery, scrubbed and chopped
1 tbsp vegetable oil
400g/14oz can chopped tomatoes
1 tbsp tomato purée
1 tsp Worcestershire sauce
salt and pepper
425g/15oz can red kidney beans, drained
2 tsp cornflour
225g/8oz aubergine, sliced
225g/8oz courgettes, sliced
175g/6oz wholemeal breadcrumbs
100g/4oz vegetarian hard cheese, grated
2 tbsp sesame seeds
2 tbsp chopped parsley
2 tsp dried basil
sliced tomatoes and parsley sprigs to garnish

Place the onion, carrot, celery and oil in a bowl. Cover and microwave at 100% (high) for 5 minutes, stirring once. Add the tomatoes, tomato purée, Worcestershire sauce and salt and pepper to taste, blending well. Microwave, uncovered, at 100% (high) for 5 minutes, stirring once. Add the kidney beans and cornflour dissolved in a little water, blending well. Microwave at 100% (high) for 2 minutes, stirring once.

Place the aubergines and courgettes in a bowl, cover and microwave at 100% (high) for 5 minutes, stirring to rearrange once. Drain well.

Mix the breadcrumbs with the cheese, sesame seeds, parsley and basil. Arrange half of the aubergine and courgette slices in a 1.5 litre/3 pint casserole. Top with half of the tomato mixture and half of the breadcrumb mixture. Repeat the layers again finishing with a layer of breadcrumbs.

Microwave at 100% (high) for 8–10 minutes, until the vegetables are tender and cooked, giving the dish a quarter turn every 2½ minutes. Brown under a preheated hot grill if liked.

Chinese Leaf Parcels

Serves: 4–6
Power setting: 100% (high)
Total cooking time: 20 minutes

10–12 large Chinese cabbage leaves
Stuffing:
½ small onion, peeled and chopped
1 garlic clove, peeled and crushed
50g/2oz celery, scrubbed and chopped
100g/4oz button mushrooms, wiped and chopped
100g/4oz fresh breadcrumbs
25g/1oz pine kernels
25g/1oz raisins
2 tbsp chopped parsley
finely grated rind of ½ lemon
1 tsp dried basil
1 egg, beaten
salt and pepper
Sauce:
2 tsp vegetable oil
50g/2oz carrot, peeled and very finely chopped
50g/2oz celery, scrubbed and finely chopped
½ small onion, peeled and finely chopped
1 garlic clove, peeled and crushed

400g/14oz can chopped tomatoes
½ tsp dried basil
pinch of sugar

Place the Chinese leaves in a large bowl. Cover and microwave at 100% (high) for 1 minute to soften. Refresh under cold running water then pat dry.

For the stuffing, place the onion, garlic, celery and mushrooms in a bowl. Cover and microwave at 100% (high) for 3 minutes, stirring once. Add the breadcrumbs, pine kernels, raisins, parsley, lemon rind, basil, egg and salt and pepper to taste and bind to a stuffing. Divide the mixture between the Chinese leaves, roll up and place seam-sides down, in a shallow cooking dish.

To make the sauce, place the oil, carrot, celery, onion and garlic in a bowl. Cover and microwave at 100% (high) for 4 minutes, stirring once. Add the tomatoes, basil, sugar and salt and pepper to taste, blending well. Microwave at 100% (high) for 3 minutes, stirring once.

Spoon over the Chinese leaf parcels, cover and microwave at 100% (high) for 5 minutes. Leave to stand for 5 minutes before serving.

Mushroom and Nut Loaf

Serves: 4–6
Power setting: 100% (high)
Total cooking time: 10–12½ minutes

100g/4oz wholemeal breadcrumbs
100g/4oz chopped mixed nuts
25g/1oz rolled oats
salt and pepper
1 egg, beaten
120ml/4fl oz vegetable stock
Filling:
25g/1oz butter or margarine
100g/4oz button mushrooms, wiped and finely sliced
1 onion, peeled and chopped
75g/3oz wholemeal breadcrumbs

1 tbsp tomato purée
1 tsp dried mixed herbs

Mix the breadcrumbs with the nuts, oats and salt and pepper to taste. Stir in the egg and stock and mix well to blend.

To make the filling, place the butter or margarine in a bowl and microwave at 100% (high) for ½ minute to melt. Add the mushrooms and onion and microwave at 100% (high) for 4 minutes until soft, stirring once. Add the breadcrumbs, tomato purée, herbs and salt and pepper to taste, blending well.

Spoon half of the nut mixture into a lightly greased 450g/1lb loaf dish. Cover with the mushroom mixture. Finish with the remaining nut mixture and level the surface. Cover with greaseproof paper, protect the ends with 5cm/2in strips of foil and microwave at 100% (high) for 6–8 minutes, removing the foil after 4 minutes, until firm and cooked, giving the dish a quarter turn every 2 minutes.

Invert on to a serving plate to serve. Serve cut into thick slices with a crisp seasonal salad.

Vegetarian Gratin

Serves: 4
Power setting: 100% (high)
Total cooking time: 16 minutes

2 medium onions, peeled and finely sliced
1 tsp dried sage
350g/12oz apples, cored and thinly sliced
675g/1½lb tomatoes, peeled and sliced
salt and pepper
350g/12oz Edam cheese, very thinly sliced
15g/½oz flaked toasted almonds

Grease a 1.2 litre/2 pint cooking dish and arrange a layer of half of the onions sprinkled with half of the sage in the bottom. Top with half of the apples and half of the tomatoes. Season generously with salt and pepper to taste then cover with half of the cheese. Repeat the layering once more, finishing with a layer of sliced cheese.

Cover and microwave at 100% (high) for 16 minutes, giving the dish a quarter turn every 4 minutes, until the vegetables are tender and the cheese is melted and bubbly. Sprinkle with the nuts and leave to stand for 3 minutes.

Brown under a preheated hot grill if liked before serving.

Vegetable and Nut Roast

Serves: 6
Power setting: 100% (high)
Total cooking time: 15–16 minutes

175g/6oz muesli with tropical fruit
175g/6oz mature Cheddar or vegetarian hard cheese, grated
salt and pepper
2 sticks celery, scrubbed and sliced
1 onion, peeled and sliced
1 tbsp oil
50g/2oz peeled potato, grated
100g/4oz salted peanuts, chopped
200g/7oz can sweetcorn with peppers, drained
230g/8oz can tomatoes
½ tsp dried oregano

Line a 1 litre/1¾ pint capacity (23 × 13cm/9 × 5in) loaf dish with cling film or greaseproof paper. Mix the muesli with the cheese and salt and pepper to taste.

Place the celery, onion and oil in a bowl. Cover and microwave at 100% (high) for 5 minutes, until soft, stirring once. Add the potato and 2 heaped tablespoons of the muesli mixture, blending well. Spoon over the base of the loaf dish and press down well. Cover with the chopped peanuts.

Mix the sweetcorn with 3 heaped tablespoons of the muesli mixture and press over the peanuts. Purée the tomatoes in a blender and add the oregano and salt and pepper to taste, blending well. Pour over the sweetcorn mixture.

Reserve 2 heaped tablespoons of the muesli mixture and

press the rest over the tomatoes. Cover loosely, stand on an upturned saucer and microwave at 100% (high) for 8 minutes, giving the dish a quarter turn every 2 minutes. Leave to stand for 5 minutes before turning out on to a serving dish.

Coat the sides and top of the loaf with the reserved muesli mixture. Return to the microwave and cook at 100% (high) for 2–3 minutes until the cheesy coating just begins to melt.

Serve hot or cold, cut into slices with a crisp salad and jacket baked potatoes.

Aubergine and Raisin Stuffed Pancakes

Serves: 4
Power setting: 100% (high)
Total cooking time: 11–13 minutes

8 cooked wholewheat pancakes
1 tbsp vegetable oil
1 onion, peeled and chopped
1cm/½in piece root ginger, peeled and grated
1 garlic clove, peeled and crushed
350g/12oz aubergine, cubed
50g/2oz raisins
75ml/3fl oz red wine
salt and pepper
150ml/¼ pint soured cream or yogurt
chopped parsley to garnish

Place the oil in a bowl with the onion, ginger and garlic. Cover and microwave at 100% (high) for 3 minutes, stirring once. Add the cubed aubergine, cover and microwave at 100% (high) for 4 minutes.

Stir in the raisins, red wine and salt and pepper to taste, blending well. Microwave, uncovered, at 100% (high) for a further 3–4 minutes, or until the aubergines are tender, stirring once. Add 1 tablespoon of the soured cream or yogurt, blending well.

Fill the pancakes evenly with the aubergine mixture and

roll up. Place, seam-sides down, in a shallow serving dish. Microwave at 100% (high) for 1–2 minutes to reheat.

Serve hot with the remaining soured cream or yogurt spooned over and sprinkled with chopped parsley.

Savoury Avocado and Walnut Risotto

Serves: 4
Power setting: 100% (high) and 50% (medium)
Total cooking time: 31½ minutes

25g/1oz butter or margarine
1 onion, peeled and sliced
1 garlic clove, peeled and crushed
2 sticks celery, scrubbed and sliced
225g/8oz long-grain brown rice
550ml/18fl oz boiling vegetable stock or water
1 tsp salt
100g/4oz button mushrooms, wiped and sliced
50g/2oz raisins
1 large ripe avocado, peeled, stoned and diced
50g/2oz walnuts, coarsely chopped
1 tbsp chopped fresh herbs
3 tbsp freshly grated Parmesan cheese or vegetarian hard cheese
freshly ground black pepper

Place the butter or margarine in a large bowl with the onion, garlic and celery. Cover and microwave at 100% (high) for 2½ minutes, stirring once. Add the rice and microwave at 100% (high) for a further 1 minute. Stir in the stock or water and salt, blending well. Cover and microwave at 100% (high) for 3 minutes.

Reduce the power setting to 50% (medium) and cook for a further 25 minutes, adding the mushrooms after 20 minutes and stirring twice. Leave to stand, covered, for 5 minutes then fluff to separate the rice grains with a fork.

Fold in the avocado, walnuts, herbs, half the cheese and pepper to taste.

Pile on to a warmed serving plate and dust with the remaining cheese. Serve at once.

Indian Summer Pasta

Serves: 4–5
Power setting: 100% (high)
Total cooking time: 11 minutes

225g/8oz dried ribbon pasta noodles
1.2 litres/2 pints boiling water
1 tbsp sunflower or groundnut oil
50g/2oz butter or margarine
2 garlic cloves, peeled and finely chopped
2 tsp ground coriander
450g/1lb tomatoes, thinly sliced
2 tsp black onion seed (optional)
450g/1lb courgettes, trimmed and sliced into thin julienne strips
¼ tsp cayenne pepper
2 tsp soft brown sugar
salt
3 tbsp fresh coriander leaves, coarsely chopped

Place the pasta in a large bowl with the boiling water and a little oil. Cover and microwave at 100% (high) for 6 minutes, stirring once. Leave to stand for 3–5 minutes then drain thoroughly.

Meanwhile, place the oil and half of the butter or margarine in a bowl and microwave at 100% (high) for ½ minute to melt. Add the garlic, coriander, tomatoes, black onion seed if used, courgettes and cayenne pepper. Microwave, uncovered, at 100% (high) for 3 minutes, stirring once.

Add the sugar, salt to taste, remaining butter and pasta, blending well. Microwave at 100% (high) for 1 minute to reheat. Stir in the coriander leaves, blending well.

Serve at once.

Cheese and Spinach Tortellini

Serves: 4–6
Power setting: 100% (high) and 50% (medium)
Total cooking time: 20 minutes

Pasta:

175g/6oz plain wholemeal or wholewheat flour
¼ tsp salt
1 egg, beaten
3 tbsp water

Filling:

100g/4oz curd or cream cheese
1 egg yolk
250g/8oz packet frozen spinach, thawed, drained and finely chopped
1 tbsp grated Parmesan cheese
¼ tsp ground nutmeg
salt and pepper
1.5 litres/2½ pints boiling water
2 tsp vegetable oil

Sauce:

15g/½oz butter or margarine
15g/½oz plain flour
200ml/7fl oz milk
3 tbsp soured cream
3 tbsp chopped parsley
1 garlic clove, peeled and crushed
salt and pepper
grated Parmesan cheese to sprinkle

To make the pasta, mix the flour with the salt. Mix the egg with the water and add to the flour to make a stiff dough. Knead until smooth, about 4 minutes then place in a greased polythene bag and leave to rest for 30 minutes.

Meanwhile to make the filling, place the cheese in a bowl and microwave at 50% (medium) for ½ minute to soften. Beat until smooth then add the egg yolk, spinach, Parmesan cheese, nutmeg and salt and pepper to taste, blending well.

Roll out the pasta, very thinly on a lightly floured surface (the pasta should be almost transparent). Using a 7cm/ 2¾in round cutter, stamp out about 40 discs of pasta. Dampen the edges with water and place a teaspoonful of the filling into the centre of each. Fold in half, seal the edges, turn up the rim and pinch the two ends of the parcel together to form a circle. Place on a floured baking tray and leave to dry for at least 30 minutes.

Cook the pasta in two batches – place half in a bowl with the boiling water and oil. Cover and microwave at 100% (high) for 8 minutes, stirring once. Leave to stand for 3 minutes then drain and place in a serving bowl. Keep warm while cooking the remaining tortellini in the drained cooking liquor. Drain well when cooked and add to the first batch of cooked tortellini.

To make the sauce, place the butter or margarine in a bowl and microwave at 100% (high) for ½ minute. Add the flour and milk, blending well. Stir in the soured cream, parsley, garlic and salt and pepper to taste, blending well. Microwave at 100% (high) for 3 minutes, until hot, smooth and thickened, stirred every 1 minute. Spoon over the tortellini and toss well to mix.

Serve at once sprinkled with grated Parmesan cheese.

Falafels with Spiced Yogurt Dip

Serves: 2
Power setting: 100% (high)
Total cooking time: 10 minutes

275g/10oz cooked chick peas (see page 15)
50g/2oz bulghur or cracked wheat, soaked in cold water for 30 minutes then squeezed dry
2 garlic cloves, peeled and finely chopped
1 tbsp wholewheat flour
1 egg, beaten
1 tbsp tahini paste
½ tsp ground coriander
½ tsp ground cumin
pinch of ground turmeric
large pinch of hot chilli powder
1 tbsp chopped fresh coriander or parsley
vegetable oil to brush
ground paprika to sprinkle
shredded lettuce to serve
Spiced yogurt dip:
150ml/¼ pint natural yogurt

1 tsp tahini paste
pinch of ground cumin
pinch of ground coriander
pinch of hot chilli powder
2 tbsp chopped fresh coriander
1 tbsp toasted sesame seeds

Purée the cooked chick peas until smooth. Add the bulghur, garlic, flour, egg, tahini paste, coriander, cumin, turmeric, chilli powder and coriander or parsley, blending well. Chill for 2 hours until very firm then divide and shape into about 20 small balls.

To cook, preheat a large browning dish according to the manufacturer's instructions, about 6 minutes at 100% (high). Lightly oil the base and add half of the falafels, arranged in a ring pattern around the edge of the dish. Sprinkle with ground paprika. Microwave at 100% (high) for 5 minutes, turning over once. Remove and repeat with the remaining falafels.

To make the dip, mix the yogurt with the tahini, cumin, coriander, chilli powder and coriander, blending well, spoon into a dish and sprinkle with the sesame seeds.

Serve chilled with the hot falafels.

Striped Vegetable Bake

Serves: 4
Power setting: 100% (high)
Total cooking time: 24–29 minutes

350g/12oz white cabbage, trimmed, cored and finely shredded
1 tbsp vegetable oil
225g/8oz carrots, peeled and very finely sliced
225g/8oz frozen asparagus spears, thawed
225g/8oz potatoes, peeled and thinly sliced
100g/4oz quark
150ml/¼ pint milk
salt and pepper
25g/1oz butter or margarine

Place the cabbage in a bowl with the oil, cover and microwave at 100% (high) for 8–9 minutes, until tender, stirring once. Spoon into a 25 × 13cm/10 × 5in shallow cooking dish. Cover with a layer of the carrots and asparagus then top with overlapping slices of the potato.

Blend the quark with the milk and salt and pepper to taste and spoon evenly over the vegetables. Dot with the butter, cover loosely and place on an inverted plate in the microwave. Microwave at 100% (high) for 16–20 minutes, giving the dish a quarter turn every 4 minutes until fork tender in the centre of the dish.

Brown under a preheated hot grill if liked before serving.

Mushroom Stroganoff

Serves: 4
Power setting: 100% (high) and 70% (medium high)
Total cooking time: 8½–11 minutes

1 tbsp safflower or sunflower oil
1 large onion, peeled and chopped
1 garlic clove, peeled and crushed
675g/1½lb button mushrooms, wiped and sliced or quartered
2 tsp ground paprika
2 tsp Worcestershire sauce
2 tbsp tomato purée
1 tbsp chopped parsley
200ml/7fl oz soured cream
salt and pepper

Place the oil, onion and garlic in a bowl. Cover and microwave at 100% (high) for 3 minutes, stirring once. Add the mushrooms, paprika, Worcestershire sauce, tomato purée and half of the parsley, blending well. Cover and microwave at 100% (high) for 4–6 minutes, stirring once, until the mushrooms are tender.

Gradually blend in all but 2 tablespoons of the soured cream and salt and pepper to taste. Reduce the power setting to 70% (medium high) and microwave for 1½–2 minutes until hot but not boiling, stirring twice.

Serve hot over boiled rice or noodles. Swirl the remaining soured cream over the mushroom mixture and sprinkle with the remaining chopped parsley.

Double-Cheese and Mushroom Spaghetti

Serves: 4
Power setting: 100% (high)
Total cooking time: 15½–18½ minutes

450g/1lb wholemeal or plain spaghetti
2 litres/3½ pints boiling water
65g/2½oz butter or margarine
100g/4oz button mushrooms, wiped and sliced
40g/1½oz plain flour
600ml/1 pint milk
100g/4oz Cotswold with chives cheese, grated or grated vegetarian hard
    cheese with 2 tsp snipped chives
salt and pepper
2 tomatoes, thinly sliced
4 tbsp grated Parmesan cheese

Place the spaghetti in a large bowl with the boiling water and hold to soften, then submerge totally. Cover loosely and microwave at 100% (high) for 10–12 minutes, stirring once. Leave to stand, covered, while preparing the sauce.

Place 25g/1oz of the butter or margarine in a bowl with the mushrooms. Cover and microwave at 100% (high) for 2 minutes, stirring once. Remove from the dish with a slotted spoon and set aside.

Add the remaining butter to the dish and microwave at 100% (high) for ½ minute to melt. Add the flour, blending well and gradually add the milk. Microwave at 100% (high) for 3–4 minutes, stirring every 1 minute, until the sauce is boiling, smooth and thickened. Add the grated cheese and salt and pepper to taste, blending well until melted and smooth.

Drain the spaghetti and add to the cheese sauce with the mushrooms. Toss gently to mix and coat.

Spoon on to 4 individual warmed serving dishes. Top each with a few slices of tomato and sprinkle with the Parmesan cheese. Serve at once with a crisp green salad.

Mixed Cheese and Broccoli Pizza

Serves: 2–3
Power setting: 100% (high)
Total cooking time: 8½–10 minutes

Base:
150g/5oz self-raising wholewheat flour
pinch of salt
25g/1oz butter or margarine
1 egg, beaten
1 tbsp milk
Topping:
15g/½oz butter or margarine
1 onion, peeled and chopped
1 tbsp tomato purée
freshly ground black pepper
2 firm tomatoes, sliced
225g/8oz cooked broccoli
50g/2oz Havarti or Samsoe cheese, grated
100g/4oz Mycella cheese, crumbled

Mix the flour with the salt. Rub in the butter or margarine until the mixture resembles fine breadcrumbs. Add the egg and milk and mix to a smooth dough. Roll out on a lightly floured surface and use to line the base of an 18cm/7in pie plate. Cover with a domed lid or inverted plate covered with greaseproof paper and microwave at 100% (high) for 3½–4 minutes, giving the plate a quarter turn every minute.

To make the topping, place the butter or margarine and onion in a bowl. Cover and microwave at 100% (high) for 3 minutes, stirring once. Add the tomato purée and pepper to taste, blending well. Spoon over the cooked base to the edges then cover with tomato slices. Top with the broccoli, broken into small florets and sprinkle with the cheeses. Microwave at 100% (high) for 2–3 minutes or until the cheese has melted and is bubbly. Brown under a preheated hot grill if liked.

Serve hot with a crunchy salad.

Cheesy Cauliflower in an Onion Crust

Serves: 4
Power setting: 100% (high)
Total cooking time: 16½–18 minutes

Pastry:
175g/6oz plain wholewheat flour
75g/3oz butter or margarine
1 small onion, peeled and grated
2–3 tbsp cold water
Filling:
225g/8oz cauliflower florets
3 tbsp water
25g/1oz butter or margarine
25g/1oz flour
300ml/½ pint milk
100g/4oz Danish Blue cheese, crumbled
freshly ground black pepper
pinch of mustard powder
1 tbsp chopped fresh parsley
2 tbsp chopped roasted peanuts

Sift the flour into a bowl, adding any bran left in the sieve. Rub in the butter or margarine until the mixture resembles fine breadcrumbs. Stir in the onion and water and bind to a pliable dough. Roll out on a lightly floured surface to a round large enough to line the base and sides of a 20cm/8in flan dish. Press in firmly, taking care not to stretch. Cut the pastry away leaving a 5mm/¼in 'collar' above the dish to allow for any shrinkage. Prick the base and sides well with a fork. Place a double thickness layer of absorbent kitchen towel over the base, easing it into position round the edges. Microwave at 100% (high) for 3½ minutes, giving the dish a quarter turn every 1 minute. Remove the paper and microwave at 100% (high) for a further 1½ minutes.

To make the filling, place the cauliflower in a bowl with the water. Cover and microwave at 100% (high) for 6–7 minutes, until tender but still crisp. Drain and reserve.

Place the butter or margarine in a bowl and microwave at 100% (high) for 1 minute to melt. Blend in the flour and milk and microwave at 100% (high) for 3½–4 minutes, stirring every 1 minute until smooth, boiling and thickened. Add the cheese, pepper to taste and mustard, blending well.

Fold the cauliflower into the cheesy sauce with the parsley. Spoon into the cooked pastry crust and microwave at 100% (high) for 1 minute. Serve warm or cold, sprinkled with the chopped peanuts. Serve with a colourful selection of young vegetables or a crisp salad.

Egg, Fruit and Vegetable Biriyani

Serves: 4
Power setting: 100% (high) and 50% (medium)
Total cooking time: 28½–29½ minutes

50g/2oz ghee, butter or margarine
25g/1oz cashews or almonds
1 onion, peeled and sliced
2 bay leaves
275g/10oz diced frozen mixed vegetables (carrots, sweetcorn, peppers, courgettes, peas and beans, for example)
1 tbsp hot Madras curry powder
1 garlic clove, peeled and crushed
225g/8oz basmati rice, washed
550ml/18fl oz boiling vegetable stock
1 tsp salt
6 dried apricots, coarsely chopped
2 tbsp raisins
4 hard-boiled eggs, shelled and cut into wedges
2 tsp garam masala
coriander sprigs to garnish

Place the ghee, butter or margarine in a large bowl and microwave at 100% (high) for 1½ minutes to melt. Add the nuts and microwave at 100% (high) for 2–3 minutes until crisp and golden, stirring once. Remove with a slotted spoon and leave to drain on absorbent kitchen towel.

Add the onion to the bowl and microwave at 100% (high) for 3 minutes, stirring once. Remove half of the onion with a slotted spoon and set aside.

Add the bay leaves, vegetables, curry powder and garlic to the onion mixture, blending well. Cover and microwave at 100% (high) for 3 minutes, stirring once. Add the rice, stock and salt, blending well. Cover and microwave at 100% (high) for 6 minutes. Reduce the power level to 50% (medium) and microwave for a further 12 minutes, stirring once.

Stir in the apricots, raisins, hard-boiled eggs and half the garam masala, blending well. Cover and leave to stand for 5 minutes.

To serve, fluff the rice with a fork to separate and place in a serving dish. Sprinkle with the remaining garam masala, the nuts and reserved onion slices. Cover and microwave at 100% (high) for 1 minute to reheat.

Serve at once garnished with sprigs of fresh coriander.

Vegan Specials

Bulghur-Stuffed Cabbage Leaves

Serves: 4
Power setting: 100% (high)
Total cooking time: 8–10 minutes

75g/3oz bulghur or cracked wheat
175ml/6fl oz boiling water
200g/7oz can red kidney beans, drained
50g/2oz raisins
3 spring onions, trimmed and chopped
50g/2oz sweetcorn kernels
1 tbsp soy sauce
salt and pepper
12 large cabbage leaves
Sauce:
400g/14oz can chopped tomatoes
1 small onion, peeled and finely chopped
1 tbsp soy sauce
chopped parsley to garnish

Place the bulghur or cracked wheat in a bowl. Pour over the boiling water and leave to stand for 10 minutes.

Meanwhile, mash the kidney beans coarsely. Add the soaked bulghur, raisins, spring onions, sweetcorn, soy sauce and salt and pepper to taste, blending well.

Place the cabbage leaves in a large bowl and microwave at 100% (high) for 2 minutes to soften, rearranging once. Place a tablespoon of the filling on to each cabbage leaf, fold over the sides and roll up to enclose the filling. Place, seam-sides down, in a shallow cooking dish.

Mix the chopped tomatoes with the onion, soy sauce and salt and pepper to taste. Pour over the cabbage leaves to coat. Cover and microwave at 100% (high) for 6–8 minutes, until cooked.

Serve hot, sprinkled with chopped parsley.

Butter Bean, Aubergine and Sunflower Seed Crunch

Serves: 4
Power setting: 100% (high)
Total cooking time: 10–11½ minutes

1 onion, peeled and finely chopped
1 tbsp vegetable oil
2 large tomatoes, chopped
450g/1lb aubergine, thinly sliced
425g/15oz can butter beans, drained
salt and pepper
120ml/4fl oz fresh wholewheat breadcrumbs
2 tbsp chopped parsley
2 tbsp sunflower seeds

Place the onion and oil in a bowl. Cover and microwave at 100% (high) for 3 minutes, until tender, stirring once. Add the tomatoes and aubergine, cover and microwave at 100% (high) for 5–5½ minutes, or until the aubergine is tender, stirring once. Stir in the butter beans with salt and pepper to taste. Spoon into a serving dish.

Mix the breadcrumbs with the parsley, sunflower seeds and salt and pepper to taste, blending well. Sprinkle over the vegetable mixture. Microwave at 100% (high) for 2–3 minutes until hot. Leave to stand for 2 minutes before serving.

Vegetarian Curry

Serves: 4
Power setting: 100% (high)
Total cooking time: 14–16 minutes

1 large potato, peeled and diced
1 onion, peeled and coarsely chopped
2 carrots, peeled and sliced diagonally
100g/4oz cauliflower florets
1 red pepper, cored, seeded and sliced
1 apple, cored and chopped

100g/4oz French beans, trimmed
2 tbsp vegetable oil
1 garlic clove, peeled and crushed
1 tbsp curry powder
1 tsp ground paprika
2 tsp tomato purée
1 tsp lemon juice
1 tbsp mango chutney
150ml/¼ pint vegetable stock
1 tomato, chopped
50g/2oz raisins or sultanas
1 tbsp toasted sunflower seeds

Place the potato, onion, carrots, cauliflower, pepper, apple, beans and oil in a large cooking dish. Cover and microwave at 100% (high) for 8–10 minutes, until tender but still crisp, stirring four times.

Add the garlic, curry powder, paprika, tomato purée, lemon juice and chutney, blending well. Gradually add the vegetable stock. Stir in the tomato and raisins or sultanas, cover and microwave at 100% (high) for 6 minutes, stirring once.

Serve hot over boiled rice sprinkled with the toasted sunflower seeds.

Courgette, Fruit and Nut Instant Couscous

Serves: 4
Power setting: 100% (high)
Total cooking time: 3–3½ minutes

2 tbsp tomato purée
1 tsp salt
1 tbsp olive oil
1 garlic clove, peeled and crushed
½ tsp ground cumin
1 tsp ground turmeric
pinch of ground coriander
100g/4oz courgettes, very coarsely shredded or finely sliced
700ml/24fl oz boiling water
225g/8oz instant medium couscous

2 tomatoes, peeled, seeded and segmented
50g/2oz raisins
50g/2oz blanched almonds
25g/1oz sunflower seeds
salt and pepper

Place the tomato purée, salt, olive oil, garlic, cumin, turmeric, coriander and courgettes in a casserole. Add the boiling water, blending well.

Add the couscous and stir well to blend. Cover and microwave at 100% (high) for 2½ minutes.

Add the tomatoes, raisins, almonds, sunflower seeds and salt and pepper to taste, blending well. Microwave at 100% (high) for ½–1 minute and serve at once.

Bulghur and Lentil Pilau

Serves: 4
Power setting: 100% (high)
Total cooking time: 22–24 minutes

50g/2oz red lentils
300ml/½ pint boiling vegetable stock
100g/4oz bulghur or cracked wheat
300ml/½ pint boiling water
1 tbsp vegetable oil
1 onion, peeled and chopped
2 sticks celery, scrubbed and chopped
1 garlic clove, peeled and crushed
1 tsp ground cumin
1 tsp ground coriander
50g/2oz raisins
25g/1oz flaked almonds
3 tomatoes, peeled and chopped
salt and pepper
1 tbsp chopped fresh coriander or parsley
almonds to garnish

Place the lentils in a bowl with the vegetable stock. Cover and microwave at 100% (high) for 15 minutes until tender, stirring twice.

Meanwhile, place the bulghur in a bowl and pour over the boiling water. Leave to stand for 10 minutes.

Place the oil in a bowl with the onion, celery, garlic, cumin and coriander. Cover and microwave at 100% (high) for 5–6 minutes, until tender, stirring once. Add the raisins, almonds, tomatoes, bulghur, lentils and salt and pepper to taste, blending well. Microwave at 100% (high) for 2–3 minutes until hot, stirring twice.

Serve hot, garnished with chopped coriander or parsley and almonds.

Fresno Chick Pea and Bean Salad

Serves: 4
Power setting: 100% (high) and 50% (medium)
Total cooking time: 30–35 minutes

225g/8oz soaked chick peas
boiling water
425g/15oz can red kidney beans, drained or 275g/10oz cooked
   red kidney beans
100g/4oz raisins
100g/4oz mushrooms, wiped and sliced
1 green pepper, cored, seeded and sliced
1 small onion, peeled and finely chopped
2 tbsp chopped parsley
2 sticks celery, scrubbed and chopped
Dressing:
225g/8oz tomatoes, peeled and finely chopped
2 tbsp vegetable oil
1 garlic clove, peeled and crushed
1 tsp ground paprika
salt and pepper

Place the chick peas in a cooking dish. Cover with boiling water. Cover and microwave at 100% (high) for 10 minutes. Reduce the power setting to 50% (medium) and cook for a further 20–25 minutes, adding extra boiling water to cover if needed, until the chick peas are tender. Drain and allow to cool.

Mix the chick peas with the kidney beans, raisins, mushrooms, green pepper, onion, parsley and celery, blending well.

Meanwhile, to make the dressing, mix the tomatoes with the oil, garlic, paprika and salt and pepper to taste. Stir into the salad mixture and toss well to coat.

Serve lightly chilled.

Warm Autumn Salad Medley with Tofu Dressing

Serves: 4–6
Power setting: 100% (high)
Total cooking time: 9 minutes

450g/1lb Jerusalem artichokes, peeled and cut into even-sized pieces
4 tbsp water
225g/8oz ripe tomatoes, peeled, seeded and chopped
50g/2oz field mushrooms, blanched and sliced
1 large courgette, trimmed and very finely sliced
50g/2oz walnuts or peanuts, coarsely chopped
1 bunch watercress, trimmed and sorted
Tofu Dressing:
175g/6oz tofu
2 tbsp lemon or lime juice
3½ tbsp corn or walnut oil
salt and pepper

Place the artichokes in a cooking dish with the water. Cover and microwave at 100% (high) for 8 minutes, until tender but still crisp, stirring once.

Add the tomatoes, mushrooms, courgette and nuts, blending well. Cover and microwave at 100% (high) for 1 minute until warm.

Meanwhile, to make the dressing, place the tofu, lemon or lime juice, oil and salt and pepper to taste in a blender and purée until smooth and creamy.

Add the watercress to the artichoke mixture, tossing well. Spoon into a serving dish and drizzle over the dressing.

Serve while still warm.

Vegetables à la Grecque

Serves: 4
Power setting: 100% (high)
Total cooking time: 17½–19½ minutes

3 tbsp tomato purée
175ml/6fl oz water
4 tbsp vegetable or olive oil
6 tbsp dry white wine
2 tsp lemon juice
1 onion, peeled and chopped
1 garlic clove, peeled and crushed
2 tsp coriander seeds
salt and pepper
1 small cauliflower, trimmed and broken into florets
2 carrots, peeled and sliced diagonally
½ red pepper, cored, seeded and sliced
½ yellow pepper, cored, seeded and sliced
100g/4oz button onions
1 stick celery, scrubbed and sliced diagonally
50g/2oz button mushrooms, wiped
2 small courgettes, wiped and sliced
50g/2oz baby French beans, trimmed and cut into 5cm/2in lengths
1 tomato, peeled and quartered
chopped parsley or coriander leaves to garnish

Place the tomato purée, water, oil, wine, lemon juice, onion, garlic, coriander seeds and salt and pepper to taste in a bowl. Cover and microwave at 100% (high) for 4½ minutes, stirring twice.

Add the cauliflower and carrots, cover and microwave at 100% (high) for 3 minutes. Add the peppers, onions and celery, blending well. Cover and microwave at 100% (high) for 6 minutes, stirring once.

Add the mushrooms, courgettes, beans and tomato, blending well. Cover and microwave at 100% (high) for 4–6 minutes or until the vegetables are tender but still crisp, stirring once. Allow to cool then chill thoroughly.

Serve cold, sprinkled with chopped parsley or coriander as a vegetable dish or delicious appetizer or light lunch dish with crusty bread.

Gourmet Vegetarian Fruit Crudités with Dips

Serves: 4
Power setting: 100% (high)
Total cooking time: 2 minutes

Dips:
225g/8oz raspberries, hulled
1 tsp honey
1 large mango, peeled, halved and stoned
1 tsp lime or lemon juice
6 tbsp blackcurrant liqueur
Crudités:
½ pineapple, peeled, cored and cubed
100g/4oz kumquats, halved
4 fresh figs, quartered
100g/4oz seedless green grapes
175g/6oz strawberries, hulled
2 passion fruit, halved
1 pear, cored and thinly sliced
1 apple, cored and thinly sliced
1 banana, peeled and sliced diagonally
4 tsp lemon juice

To make the dips, place the raspberries and honey in a bowl. Cover and microwave at 100% (high) for 2 minutes, stirring once. Allow to cool then purée in a blender then pass through a fine sieve to remove the pips. Place in a small serving bowl. Purée the mango in a blender with the lime or lemon juice and place in a small serving bowl. Pour the blackcurrant liqueur into a small serving bowl.

Arrange the pineapple, kumquats, figs, grapes, strawberries and passion fruit around the edge of a large plate. Toss the pear, apple and banana in the lemon juice and add to the plate. Place the prepared dips in the centre to serve.

Vegan Chilli

Serves: 4
Power setting: 100% (high) and 50% (medium)
Total cooking time: 17–20 minutes

2 tbsp vegetable oil
1 onion, peeled and chopped
225g/8oz bulghur grains
2 × 400g/14oz cans chopped tomatoes
2 tsp chilli seasoning
1 tsp tomato purée
225g/8oz soaked red kidney beans, cooked (see page 24)
salt and pepper

Place the oil and onion in a large bowl. Cover and
microwave at 100% (high) for 3 minutes, stirring once.
Add the bulghur and microwave at 100% (high) for 2
minutes, stirring once. Add the tomatoes, chilli seasoning,
tomato purée, cooked beans and salt and pepper to taste,
blending well.

Cover and microwave at 100% (high) for 3 minutes.
Reduce the power level to 50% (medium) and microwave
for a further 9–12 minutes until tender, stirring twice. It
may be necessary to add a little extra hot water or vegetable
stock to the mixture if the tomatoes are of the thick and
chunky variety.

Serve hot with tortilla chips or warm crackers.

Versatile Vegetables, Grains and Salads

Gingered Carrot and Courgette Julienne

Serves: 4
Power setting: 100% (high)
Total cooking time: 5–6 minutes

3 large carrots, peeled and cut into thin julienne strips
1 tbsp grated root ginger
1 tbsp orange juice
15g/½oz butter or margarine
2 courgettes, trimmed and cut into thin julienne strips
2 tbsp chopped parsley
salt and pepper

Place the carrots, ginger, orange juice and butter or margarine in a cooking dish. Cover and microwave at 100% (high) for 3 minutes, stirring once.

Add the courgettes, parsley and salt and pepper to taste, blending well. Cover and microwave at 100% (high) for 2–3 minutes, until the vegetables are tender but crisp. Leave to stand, covered, for 3 minutes before serving.

Root Vegetable Dauphinoise

Serves: 4
Power setting: 100% (high)
Total cooking time: 14 minutes

900g/2lb old potatoes, peeled and thinly sliced
2 carrots, peeled and thinly sliced
1 large parsnip, peeled and thinly sliced
2 tbsp water
85g/3oz packet full-fat soft cheese
5 tbsp milk
salt and pepper
2 tbsp grated Parmesan or vegetarian hard cheese
1 tbsp snipped chives
parsley sprigs to garnish

Layer the potatoes, carrots and parsnip in a shallow cooking dish. Add the water, cover and microwave at 100% (high) for 10 minutes, or until the vegetables are just fork tender.

Mix the cheese with the milk and salt and pepper to taste. Pour over the vegetable mixture and sprinkle with the remaining cheese and chives. Microwave at 100% (high) for a further 4 minutes. Leave to stand for 3–5 minutes before serving garnished with parsley sprigs. If liked, brown under a preheated hot grill before serving.

Sun-kissed Leeks and Fennel

Serves: 4
Power setting: 100% (high)
Total cooking time: 14–16 minutes

1 large onion, peeled and chopped
225g/8oz leeks, washed and sliced lengthways into fine strips
225g/8oz fennel, trimmed and sliced
1 garlic clove, peeled and crushed
2 tbsp fruity olive oil
100ml/4fl oz dry white wine
4 medium ripe tomatoes, peeled, seeded and chopped
1 tbsp tomato purée
1½ tsp chopped fresh mixed herbs
salt and pepper
chopped parsley to garnish

Place the onion, leeks, fennel and garlic in a bowl, blending well. Mix the oil with the wine, tomatoes, tomato purée, herbs and salt and pepper to taste. Pour over the fennel mixture and mix well to coat.

Cover and microwave at 100% (high) for 14–16 minutes, stirring twice, until tender and well blended. Serve warm or cool, then chill and serve sprinkled with chopped parsley. A delicious vegetable side dish or vegetable starter to serve with crusty warm wholemeal bread.

Lemon-zested Celery, Lettuce Heart and Peas

Serves: 4
Power setting: 100% (high)
Total cooking time: 12–14 minutes

1 head celery, scrubbed and sliced
½ onion, peeled and sliced
25g/1oz butter or margarine
2 tbsp water
grated rind of ½ lemon
salt
225g/8oz frozen peas
2 lettuce hearts, quartered
1 tbsp snipped chives

Place the celery, onion, butter or margarine, water, lemon rind and salt to taste in a bowl. Cover and microwave at 100% (high) for 6 minutes, stirring once.

Add the peas, blending well. Cover and microwave at 100% (high) for 4 minutes. Add the lettuce hearts and chives, blending well. Cover and microwave at 100% (high) for 2–4 minutes, or until cooked and tender but not limp, stirring once. Allow to stand for 3 minutes before serving.

Mushroom and Spinach Bake

Serves: 4
Power setting: 100% (high)
Total cooking time: 15–18 minutes

275g/10oz packet frozen leaf or chopped spinach
pinch of ground nutmeg
salt and pepper
225g/8oz button mushrooms, wiped and halved
40g/1½oz butter or margarine
40g/1½oz plain flour
450ml/¾ pint milk
100g/4oz vegetarian hard cheese, grated

Place the spinach in a bowl. Cover and microwave at 100%

(high) for 7–9 minutes, stirring to break up twice. Add the nutmeg and salt and pepper to taste and spoon into a shallow dish.

Place the mushrooms and butter or margarine in a bowl. Cover and microwave at 100% (high) for 3 minutes, stirring once. Remove with a slotted spoon and spoon over the spinach.

Add the flour to the mushrooom juices, blending well. Gradually add the milk. Microwave at 100% (high) for 3–4 minutes, stirring every 1 minute, until the sauce is boiling, smooth and thickened. Stir in three-quarters of the cheese with salt and pepper to taste. Spoon over the mushrooms and spinach and sprinkle with the remaining cheese.

Microwave at 100% (high) for about 2 minutes or until the cheese melts. Brown under a preheated hot grill if liked.

Leek, Horseradish and Cheese-filled Potatoes

Serves: 4
Power setting: 100% (high)
Total cooking time: 18–22 minutes

4 × 175g/6oz potatoes, scrubbed
225g/8oz leeks, trimmed and sliced
2 tbsp water
2 tbsp thick set natural yogurt
2 tsp horseradish relish
1 tbsp chopped parsley
100g/4oz vegetarian hard cheese, grated
salt and pepper

Prick the potato skins and place on a double sheet of absorbent kitchen towel. Microwave at 100% (high) for 12–15 minutes, turning over once. Leave to stand for 4 minutes then cut in halves and scoop out the cooked flesh into a bowl.

Meanwhile, place the leek and water in a bowl. Cover and microwave at 100% (high) for 4–5 minutes until cooked, stirring once. Drain thoroughly and mix with the potato, mashing well to blend. Add the yogurt, horseradish, half the parsley and cheese and salt and pepper to taste.

Pile the filling back into the potato shells and sprinkle with the remaining cheese. Microwave at 100% (high) for 2 minutes to reheat. Brown under a preheated hot grill if liked.

Serve hot, garnished with the remaining chopped parsley.

Sizzled Sage Courgettes

Serves: 4
Power setting: 100% (high)
Total cooking time: 6–8 minutes

1 tbsp oil
small knob of butter or margarine
1 small garlic clove, peeled and finely chopped
450g/1lb courgettes, topped and tailed and thinly sliced or cut into thin
    julienne strips
1 tbsp chopped fresh sage
salt and pepper
½ tsp grated lemon rind
2 tsp lemon juice

Preheat a large browning dish according to the manufacturer's instructions, about 6 minutes at 100% (high) adding the oil and butter or margarine for the last ½ minute.

Add the garlic, courgettes and sage, pressing down well to brown lightly. Cover and microwave at 100% (high) for 6–8 minutes, stirring twice.

Season to taste with salt and pepper, stir in the lemon rind and juice, cover and leave to stand for 2 minutes before serving.

Ratatouille

Serves: 4
Power setting: 100% (high)
Total cooking time: 21 minutes

2 tbsp olive oil
2 onions, peeled and sliced
1 garlic clove, peeled and crushed
1 small red pepper, cored, seeded and sliced
1 small yellow pepper, cored, seeded and sliced
175g/6oz courgettes, trimmed and sliced
1 small aubergine, cubed
450g/1lb tomatoes, peeled, seeded and quartered
salt and pepper
chopped parsley to garnish
grated Parmesan to serve (optional)

Place the oil, onions, garlic and peppers in a bowl. Cover and microwave at 100% (high) for 6 minutes, stirring once.

Add the courgettes, aubergine, tomatoes and salt and pepper to taste, blending well. Cover and microwave at 100% (high) for 10 minutes, stirring once. Remove the cover and microwave at 100% (high) for 5 minutes, stirring once.

Serve hot or cold, sprinkled with chopped parsley to garnish. If liked the ratatouille can be sprinkled with grated Parmesan cheese for serving. Serve as a vegetable accompaniment or starter dish with crusty wholemeal bread.

Parchment Baked Mushroom and Cherry Tomato Sizzles

Serves: 4
Power setting: 100% (high)
Total cooking time: 6 minutes

1 tbsp melted butter, margarine or oil
100g/4oz field mushrooms or ceps, wiped and sliced
100g/4oz cherry tomatoes, halved
100g/4oz baby courgettes, trimmed and sliced lengthways

1 stick celery, scrubbed and chopped
25g/1oz pine nuts
1 tbsp chopped fresh basil
½ tsp Dijon mustard
salt and pepper

Cut four large squares of greaseproof paper and lightly brush with the butter, margarine or oil.

Mix the mushrooms with the tomatoes, courgettes, celery, pine nuts, basil, mustard and salt and pepper to taste, blending well. Divide the mixture evenly between the sheets of greaseproof paper and fold over or gather up to enclose. Secure with an elastic band if liked to keep tight.

Microwave at 100% (high) for 6 minutes, rearranging once. Serve in their parchment wrapping for opening at the table.

Oriental Mushroom and Tofu Express

Serves: 2–4
Power setting: 100% (high) and 20% (defrost)
Total cooking time: 12–15 minutes

2 tbsp sesame oil
½ bunch spring onions, trimmed and chopped
1cm/½in piece root ginger, peeled and grated
1 garlic clove, peeled and crushed
350g/12oz mushrooms, wiped
120ml/4fl oz vegetable stock
1 tbsp soy sauce
4 tbsp black bean, yellow bean or oyster sauce
2 tsp cornflour
2 tbsp water
175g/6oz tofu, cubed and fried until golden if liked

Place half the oil, spring onions, ginger and garlic in a bowl. Cover and microwave at 100% (high) for 1 minute. Add the mushrooms, blending well. Cover and microwave at 100% (high) for 3 minutes, stirring once.

Add the stock, soy sauce, black bean, yellow bean or oyster sauce and cornflour blended with the water. Cover and microwave at 20% (defrost) for 7–9 minutes, stirring 3 times.

Add the tofu and microwave at 100% (high) for 1–2 minutes to reheat.

Serve at once drizzled with the remaining sesame oil.

Wild Rice, Cashew and Mushroom Timbales

Serves: 4
Power setting: 100% (high)
Total cooking time: 36–38 minutes

100g/4oz wild rice
2 tbsp vegetable oil
600ml/1 pint boiling water
salt and pepper
25g/1oz currants
1 onion, peeled and finely chopped
100g/4oz mushrooms, wiped and chopped
25g/1oz salted cashew nuts, coarsely chopped
12–16 fresh spinach leaves, trimmed

Soak the wild rice in 600ml/1 pint warm water for 2–3 hours. Drain thoroughly then place in a bowl with 1 tablespoon of the oil, the boiling water and salt and pepper to taste. Cover and microwave at 100% (high) for 30 minutes, stirring once. Add the currants and leave to stand, covered, for 5 minutes.

Meanwhile, place the remaining oil and onion in a bowl and microwave at 100% (high) for 2 minutes. Add the mushrooms and microwave for a further 2–3 minutes until the onion and mushrooms are tender.

Stir into the rice mixture with the nuts and salt and pepper to taste, blending well.

Place the spinach in a bowl, cover and microwave at 100% (high) for 1 minute to soften. Refresh under cold running water and pat dry. Use to line 4 well-oiled ramekin or timbale dishes. Spoon in the rice mixture, packing down well and fold over the spinach leaves to enclose. Cover with vented cling film and microwave at 100% (high) for 1–2 minutes to reheat.

Unmould on to plates to serve. Delicious with vegetable hotpots and curries.

Kasha

Serves: 6
Power setting: 100% (high) and 50% (medium)
Total cooking time: 15½–17½ minutes

50g/2oz butter or margarine
2 eggs, beaten
450g/1lb pre-roasted buckwheat
600ml/1 pint boiling vegetable stock
salt and pepper
1 onion, peeled and finely sliced
chopped parsley to garnish

Place half the butter in a bowl and microwave at 100% (high) for ½ minute to melt. Add the egg and buckwheat and beat well to blend. Cook, uncovered, at 100% (high) for 2 minutes, stirring three times to separate the grains.

Add the stock and salt and pepper to taste, blending well. Cover and microwave at 100% (high) for 3 minutes.

Add the onion, reduce the power setting to 50% (medium) and cook for a further 10–12 minutes or until the buckwheat is tender, stirring 2–3 times. Fluff with a fork before serving, topped with the remaining butter or margarine and sprinkled with chopped parsley.

Mangetout and Salad Finery in Buttery Avocado Dressing

Serves: 4
Power setting: 100% (high)
Total cooking time: 3–4 minutes

1 tbsp olive oil
1 small red onion, peeled and sliced into rings

100g/4oz mangetout, trimmed
1 green pepper, cored, seeded and chopped
75g/3oz curly endive or frisée, trimmed and torn into pieces
75g/3oz feuille de chêne or batavia lettuce, trimmed and torn into pieces
25g/1oz corn salad, trimmed
¼ Cos lettuce, shredded
¼ cucumber, cut into thin julienne strips
1 avocado, peeled, stoned and cubed
Dressing:
2 tbsp virgin olive oil
1 tsp wholegrain mustard
2 tsp tarragon or white wine vinegar
1 tbsp chopped fresh herbs (tarragon, parsley, chives, chervil or basil, for
  example)
salt and pepper

Place the oil in a bowl with the onion and mangetout. Cover
and microwave at 100% (high) for 2 minutes, stirring once.
Allow to cool.

Place the pepper, curly endive or frisée, feuille de chêne
or batavia lettuce, corn salad, Cos lettuce, cucumber and
avocado in a large salad bowl. Add the onion and mangetout
mixture and toss well to blend.

Place the dressing ingredients in a jar and shake well to
blend. Pour over the salad and toss well to coat. Cover and
microwave at 100% (high) for 1–2 minutes or until the
avocado starts to melt and the dressing is warm but the
salad mixture is still crisp.

Toss again to mix and serve while still warm.

Piquant Wholewheat Pasta Salad

Serves: 4
Power setting: 100% (high)
Total cooking time: 12–14 minutes

225g/8oz wholewheat pasta wheat ears or other small shapes
1.2 litres/2 pints boiling water
½ tsp vegetable oil
1 red pepper, cored, seeded and chopped
175g/6oz cooked sweetcorn kernels

100g/4oz raisins
2 tbsp chopped parsley
3 tbsp mayonnaise
3 tbsp apple purée
salt and pepper

Place the pasta in a large bowl with the boiling water and oil. Cover and microwave at 100% (high) for 12–14 minutes, stirring once. Leave to stand for 3 minutes, then drain and refresh under cold running water.

Mix the cool pasta with the red pepper, sweetcorn, raisins and parsley. Mix the mayonnaise with the apple purée and salt and pepper to taste. Pour over the salad and toss well to blend.

Serve lightly chilled.

Concertina Salad

Serves: 4
Power setting: 50% (medium)
Total cooking time: ½–1 minute

4 large beefsteak tomatoes
4 hard-boiled eggs, shelled and sliced
225g/8oz Edam cheese, sliced
225g/8oz cucumber, sliced
85g/3oz packet soft cheese with chives
3 tbsp natural yogurt or low-fat mayonnaise
salt and pepper

Place each tomato, stalk end down, on an individual serving plate and make 6 parallel downward cuts almost to the base of each. Fill each cut slice with a piece of egg and cheese. Arrange the cucumber slices around the bases of the tomatoes.

To make the dressing, place the soft cheese in a bowl and microwave at 50% (medium) for ½–1 minute until softened and creamy, beating well. Stir in the yogurt or mayonnaise and season with salt and pepper to taste. Spoon across the centre of each tomato to serve.

Cheesy Waldorf Salad

Serves: 6
Power setting: 50% (medium)
Total cooking time: ½–1 minute

2 tbsp lemon juice
1 tsp castor sugar
1 tbsp mayonnaise
450g/1lb green eating apples, cored and diced
4 sticks celery, scrubbed and chopped
100g/4oz seedless green grapes
50g/2oz walnuts, chopped
100g/4oz Danish Blue Castello cheese or other soft, mild, blue-veined
  cheese
6 tbsp natural yogurt
salt and pepper
celery leaves to garnish

Mix the lemon juice with the sugar and the mayonnaise. Add the apples and toss well to coat. Add the celery, grapes and walnuts, blending well.

Place the cheese in a bowl and microwave at 50% (medium) for ½–1 minute until softened. Beat in the yogurt and salt and pepper to taste to make a thick and smooth dressing. Pour over the apple mixture and toss well to coat.

Spoon on to a serving plate and garnish with celery leaves.

Curried Rice and Vegetable Salad

Serves: 4
Power setting: 100% (high) and 50% (medium)
Total cooking time: 23–28 minutes

100g/4oz long-grain brown rice
300ml/½ pint boiling water
salt and pepper
1 tbsp mayonnaise
1 tbsp mango chutney
1 tsp shredded dried coconut

225g/8oz can curried beans
1 small red pepper, cored, seeded and sliced
¼ cucumber, sliced
4 dried apricots, chopped
coriander or parsley sprigs to garnish

Place the rice, boiling water and ½ teaspoon of salt in a large cooking dish. Cover and microwave at 100% (high) for 3 minutes. Reduce the power setting to 50% (medium) and cook for a further 20–25 minutes, stirring twice, until the rice is cooked and all the water has been absorbed. Leave to stand, covered, for 5 minutes then fluff with a fork to separate and leave to cool.

Meanwhile, blend the mayonnaise with the chutney and coconut. Add the curried beans, pepper, cucumber, apricots and cooked rice, mixing well.

Spoon on to a serving plate and garnish with sprigs of parsley or coriander. Serve with wholemeal pitta bread.

Barbecue Bean, Pasta and Cheese Salad

Serves: 4
Power setting: 100% (high)
Total cooking time: 2–3 minutes

225g/8oz fresh wholewheat pasta shapes
750ml/1¼ pints boiling water
1 tsp vegetable oil
salt and pepper
1 tsp wholegrain mustard
2 tsp wine vinegar
4 spring onions, trimmed and chopped
450g/1lb can barbecue beans
100g/4oz Cheddar or vegetarian hard cheese, cut into julienne strips
100g/4oz fresh bean sprouts, rinsed
lettuce leaves to serve
chopped parsley to garnish

Place the pasta in a large bowl with the water, oil and a pinch of salt, blending well. Cover and microwave at 100%

(high) for 2–3 minutes. Drain, refresh under cold running water and drain again.

Meanwhile, blend the mustard with the vinegar. Add the spring onions, barbecue beans, cheese and bean sprouts, blending well. Stir in the cooked pasta and salt and pepper to taste, then pile on to a serving plate lined with lettuce leaves.

Serve lightly chilled, garnished with chopped parsley.

Salad Primavera

Serves: 4
Power setting: 100% (high)
Total cooking time: 16–18 minutes

75g/3oz broccoli, broken into small florets
75g/3oz fine young green beans, trimmed and cut into short lengths
2 tbsp water
75g/3oz pasta spirals
600ml/1 pint boiling water
2 spring onions, trimmed and chopped
50g/2oz black olives
2 gherkins, chopped
Dressing:
2 tsp wholegrain mustard powder
1 tbsp lemon juice
3 tbsp sunflower oil
salt and pepper

Place the broccoli and beans in a bowl with the water. Cover and microwave at 100% (high) for 4 minutes, stirring once, until cooked and tender. Drain and allow to cool.

Meanwhile, place the pasta and boiling water in a bowl. Cover and microwave at 100% (high) for 12–14 minutes, until tender, stirring once. Leave to stand for 3 minutes then drain thoroughly and allow to cool.

Mix the cooked pasta with the broccoli, beans, spring onions, olives and gherkins in a serving bowl. Place all the dressing ingredients in a small bowl and beat well to combine. Pour over the salad and toss well to coat. Serve as soon as possible.

Pink Summer Salad

Serves: 4
Power setting: 100% (high)
Total cooking time: 1½ minutes

75g/3oz mangetout, trimmed and sliced
1 tbsp water
1 small endive or curly lettuce, torn into small pieces
1 pink grapefruit, peeled, pith removed and segmented
1 yellow pepper, cored, seeded and sliced
2 tsp snipped chives
1 tbsp toasted pumpkin or sunflower seeds
Dressing:
2 tsp wholegrain mustard
1 tbsp fresh pink grapefruit juice
3 tbsp sunflower oil
salt and pepper

Place the mangetout and water in a bowl. Cover and microwave at 100% (high) for 1½ minutes. Drain and leave to cool.

Place the endive or lettuce, mangetout, grapefruit, pepper and chives in a serving bowl. Mix the mustard powder with the grapefruit juice, oil and salt and pepper to taste, blending well. Pour over the salad mixture and toss well to coat.

Serve sprinkled with the pumpkin or sunflower seeds.

A – Z of Microwave Vegetable Cooking

A

Artichokes

GLOBE   Discard the tough, outer leaves. Snip the tips off the remaining leaves and trim the stems to the base. Wash and shake to remove excess water, stand upright in a cooking dish. Pour over water (or stock) and lemon juice. Cover and cook for the time specified, basting and rearranging twice. Test if cooked at the minimum time – try to pull a leaf from the base, if it comes away freely the artichoke is cooked. Leave to stand, covered, for 5 minutes before serving.

Quantity	Water	Lemon juice	Power	Minutes
1	6 tbsp	1½ tsp	100% (high)	5–6
2	8 tbsp	1 tbsp	100% (high)	10–11
4	150ml/¼ pint	2 tbsp	100% (high)	15–18

JERUSALEM   Peel and cut into even-sized pieces. Place in a cooking dish with the water or butter. Cover and cook for the time specified, stirring once. Leave to stand, covered, for 3 minutes before serving.

Quantity	Water	or	Butter	Power	Minutes
450g/1lb	4 tbsp		25g/1oz	100% (high)	8–10

Asparagus

FRESH WHOLE SPEARS   Prepare and arrange in a large shallow dish with pointed tips to the centre. Add water, cover and cook for time specified, rearranging spears but still keeping tips to centre after half of the time.

Quantity	Water	Power	Minutes
450g/1lb	125ml/4½fl oz	100% (high)	12–14

FRESH CUT SPEARS Prepare and place in a large shallow dish. Add water, cover and cook for time specified, stirring once.

Quantity	Water	Power	Minutes
450g/1lb	125ml/4½fl oz	100% (high)	9–11

FROZEN WHOLE SPEARS Place in a cooking dish with water. Cover and cook for time specified, rearranging once. Leave to stand for 5 minutes before serving.

Quantity	Water	Power	Minutes
450g/1lb	125ml/4½fl oz	100% (high)	9–12

CANNED WHOLE SPEARS Drain and place in a cooking dish. Cover and cook for time specified, rearranging once.

Quantity	Power	Minutes
1 × 425g/15oz can	100% (high)	3–4

CANNED CUT SPEARS Drain and place in a cooking dish. Cover and cook for time specified, rearranging once.

Quantity	Power	Minutes
1 × 300g/11oz can	100% (high)	2–2½

Aubergines

FRESH CUBES Cut unpeeled aubergine into 2cm/¾in cubes. Place in a cooking dish with butter. Cover and cook for time specified, stirring every 3 minutes. Leave to stand, covered, for 4 minutes. Season after cooking.

Quantity	Butter	Power	Minutes
450g/1lb	25g/1oz	100% (high)	7–10

FRESH WHOLE Peel off stalks, rinse and dry. Brush with a little oil and prick. Place on absorbent kitchen towel and cook for time specified, turning once. Leave to stand for 4 minutes. Scoop out flesh and use as required.

Quantity	Power	Minutes
1 × 225g/8oz	100% (high)	3–4
2 × 225g/8oz	100% (high)	4–6

FROZEN SLICES   Place in a shallow dish. Cover and cook for time specified, stirring 2–3 times. Drain and pat dry to use.

Quantity	Power	Minutes
225g/8oz	20% (defrost)	7
450g/1lb	20% (defrost)	10–13

B

Beans

FRESH GREEN   Place whole or cut beans in a bowl with the water. Cover and cook for the time specified, stirring once. Leave to stand, covered, for 2–3 minutes before serving.

Quantity	Water	Power	Minutes
225g/8oz whole	2 tbsp	100% (high)	8–10
450g/1lb whole	2 tbsp	100% (high)	15–18
225g/8oz cut	2 tbsp	100% (high)	7–9
450g/1lb cut	2 tbsp	100% (high)	12–15

FRESH BABY GREEN WHOLE OR FRENCH WHOLE   Place in a bowl with the water. Cover and cook for the time specified, stirring 3 times. Leave to stand, covered, for 2–3 minutes before serving.

Quantity	Water	Power	Minutes
225g/8oz	2 tbsp	100% (high)	7–9
450g/1lb	2 tbsp	100% (high)	12–15

FRESH SLICED RUNNER BEANS   Place in a bowl with the water. Cover and cook for the time specified, stirring 3–4 times. Leave to stand, covered, for 2–3 minutes before serving.

Quantity	Water	Power	Minutes
225g/8oz	2 tbsp	100% (high)	7–9
450g/1lb	2 tbsp	100% (high)	12–15

FRESH SHELLED BROAD BEANS   Place in a bowl with the water. Cover and cook for the time specified, stirring once. Leave to stand, covered, for 2–3 minutes before serving.

Quantity	Water	Power	Minutes
225g/8oz	5 tbsp	100% (high)	5–7
450g/1lb	100ml/4fl oz	100% (high)	6–10

FROZEN GREEN BEANS   Place in a bowl with the water. Cover and cook for the time specified, stirring once. Leave to stand, covered, for 2–3 minutes before serving.

Quantity	Water	Power	Minutes
225g/8oz whole	2 tbsp	100% (high)	9–10
450g/1lb whole	4 tbsp	100% (high)	14–15
225g/8oz cut	2 tbsp	100% (high)	6–7
450g/1lb cut	4 tbsp	100% (high)	10–12

FROZEN BABY GREEN WHOLE OR FRENCH WHOLE   Place in a bowl with the water. Cover and cook for the time specified, stirring 3 times. Leave to stand, covered, for 2–3 minutes before serving.

Quantity	Water	Power	Minutes
225g/8oz	2 tbsp	100% (high)	8–9
450g/1lb	4 tbsp	100% (high)	13–15

FROZEN SLICED RUNNER BEANS   Place in a bowl with the water. Cover and cook for the time specified, stirring twice. Leave to stand, covered, for 2–3 minutes before serving.

Quantity	Water	Power	Minutes
225g/8oz	2 tbsp	100% (high)	6–7
450g/1lb	4 tbsp	100% (high)	10–12

FROZEN SHELLED BROAD BEANS Place in a bowl with the water. Cover and cook for the time specified, stirring twice. Leave to stand, covered, for 2–3 minutes before serving.

Quantity	Water	Power	Minutes
225g/8oz	4 tbsp	100% (high)	6–7
450g/1lb	100ml/4fl oz	100% (high)	10–11

CANNED GREEN AND BROAD BEANS Drain all but liquid specified. Place in a cooking dish with the liquid. Cover and cook for time specified, stirring once.

Quantity	Liquid	Power	Minutes
1 × 280g/10oz can whole green	2 tbsp	100% (high)	2–3
2 × 280g/10oz cans whole green	2 tbsp	100% (high)	4–5
1 × 280g/10oz can cut green	2 tbsp	100% (high)	2–3
2 × 280g/10oz cans cut green	2 tbsp	100% (high)	4–4½
1 × 280g/10oz can broad	2 tbsp	100% (high)	2
2 × 280g/10oz cans broad	2 tbsp	100% (high)	3

Beetroot

FRESH Wash the beetroot and pierce the skin with a fork but do not peel. Place in a shallow dish with the water, cover loosely and cook for the time specified, rearranging twice. Leave to stand, covered, for 5 minutes before removing skins to serve or use.

Quantity	Water	Power	Minutes
4 medium	3–4 tbsp	100% (high)	14–16

Broccoli

FRESH SPEARS Place spears in a large shallow dish with tender heads to centre of dish. Add water, cover with a lid or vented cling film. Cook for time specified, rotating dish once. Leave to stand, covered, for 2–4 minutes before serving.

Quantity	Water	Power	Minutes
225g/8oz	4 tbsp	100% (high)	4–5
450g/1lb	4 tbsp	100% (high)	8–9

FRESH PIECES Cut into 2.5cm/1in pieces. Place in a large dish. Add water, cover and cook for time specified, stirring once. Leave to stand, covered, for 3–5 minutes before serving.

Quantity	Water	Power	Minutes
225g/8oz	4 tbsp	100% (high)	4½–5
450g/1lb	4 tbsp	100% (high)	8½–9½

FROZEN SPEARS Place in a cooking dish with water. Cover and cook for time specified, stirring once. Leave to stand for 2–3 minutes before serving.

Quantity	Water	Power	Minutes
1 × 250g/9oz packet	4 tbsp	100% (high)	7–8
2 × 250g/9oz packets	4 tbsp	100% (high)	14–15

Brussels Sprouts

FRESH Remove outer leaves, trim and cross-cut base. Place in a cooking dish with the water. Cover and cook for the time specified, stirring once. Leave to stand, covered, for 3–5 minutes before serving.

Quantity	Water	Power	Minutes
450g/1lb	4 tbsp	100% (high)	6–7
900g/2lb	8 tbsp	100% (high)	12–14

FROZEN Place in a cooking dish with the water. Cover and cook for the time specified, stirring once. Leave to stand, covered, for 3–5 minutes before serving.

Quantity	Water	Power	Minutes
450g/1lb	2 tbsp	100% (high)	10–11
900g/2lb	4 tbsp	100% (high)	20–22

C

Cabbage

FRESH Core and shred and place in a large dish so that the cabbage fits loosely. Add water, cover and cook for the specified time, stirring once. Leave to stand for 2 minutes before serving. Season after cooking.

Quantity	Water	Power	Minutes
225g/8oz	4 tbsp	100% (high)	7–9
450g/1lb	8 tbsp	100% (high)	9–11

FROZEN Place in a large dish with the water. Cover and cook for the specified time, stirring once. Leave to stand for 2 minutes before serving. Season after cooking.

Quantity	Water	Power	Minutes
225g/8oz	4 tbsp	100% (high)	6–8
450g/1lb	8 tbsp	100% (high)	8–10

Carrots

FRESH BABY WHOLE AND SLICED Place in a cooking dish with the water. Cover and cook for the time specified, stirring once. Leave to stand, covered, for 3–5 minutes before serving.

Quantity	Water	Power	Minutes
450g/1lb whole	4 tbsp	100% (high)	12–14
450g/1lb sliced	4 tbsp	100% (high)	10–12

FROZEN BABY WHOLE AND SLICED Place in a cooking dish with the water. Cover and cook for the time specified, stirring once. Leave to stand, covered, for 2–3 minutes before serving.

Quantity	Water	Power	Minutes
450g/1lb whole	2 tbsp	100% (high)	10–12
450g/1lb sliced	2 tbsp	100% (high)	8–10

Cauliflower

FRESH WHOLE   Trim but leave whole and place, floret side down, in a dish with the water. Cover and cook for the time specified, turning over once. Leave to stand for 3–5 minutes before serving.

Quantity	Water	Power	Minutes
1 × 675g/1½lb whole	8 tbsp	50% (medium)	13–17

FRESH FLORETS   Place in a dish with the water. Cover and cook for the time specified, stirring once. Leave to stand for 3 minutes before serving.

Quantity	Water	Power	Minutes
225g/8oz	3 tbsp	100% (high)	7–8
450g/1lb	4 tbsp	100% (high)	10–12

FROZEN FLORETS   To thaw and cook, place in a dish with the water. Cover and cook for the time specified, stirring once. Leave to stand for 2–3 minutes before serving.

Quantity	Water	Power	Minutes
225g/8oz	3 tbsp	100% (high)	5–6
450g/1lb	4 tbsp	100% (high)	8–9

Celery

FRESH SLICED   Slice into 5mm/¼in pieces and place in a shallow cooking dish. Add water and butter, cover and cook for the time specified, stirring once. Leave to stand, covered, for 3 minutes before serving.

Quantity	Water	Butter	Power	Minutes
1 head/9 large sticks	2 tbsp	25g/1oz	100% (high)	5–6

FRESH CELERY HEARTS   Halve each heart lengthways and place in a shallow cooking dish. Add water and knob of butter if liked. Cover and cook for the time specified, turning once. Leave to stand, covered, for 3 minutes before serving.

Quantity	Water	Power	Minutes
4 hearts	2 tbsp	100% (high)	4½–5

Chinese Cabbage

FRESH   Slice and place in a large dish so that the cabbage fits loosely. Add water, cover and cook for the time specified, stirring once. Leave to stand for 3–5 minutes before serving. Season after cooking.

Quantity	Water	Power	Minutes
450g/1lb	2–3 tbsp	100% (high)	6–8

Corn on the Cob and Corn Kernels

FRESH UNHUSKED   Arrange on the base of the cooker or on turntable, evenly spaced. Cook for the time specified, rotating and rearranging once. Leave to stand for 5 minutes before removing husk, silky threads and woody base with a sharp knife.

Quantity	Power	Minutes
1 × 175–225g/6–8oz	100% (high)	3–5
2 × 175–225g/6–8oz	100% (high)	6–8
3 × 175–225g/6–8oz	100% (high)	8–10
4 × 175–225g/6–8oz	100% (high)	10–12

FRESH HUSKED   Wrap individually in cling film or place in a dish with 4 tbsp water and cover. Place or arrange evenly in the microwave and cook for the time specified, rotating and rearranging once. Leave to stand, covered, for 3–5 minutes before serving.

Quantity	Power	Minutes
1 × 175–225g/6–8oz	100% (high)	3–4
2 × 175–225g/6–8oz	100% (high)	5–6
3 × 175–225g/6–8oz	100% (high)	7–8
4 × 175–225g/6–8oz	100% (high)	9–10

FROZEN CORN KERNELS Place in a cooking dish with 4 tbsp water. Cover and cook for the time specified, stirring once. Leave to stand, covered, for 2–3 minutes before serving.

Quantity	Power	Minutes
1 × 283g/10oz packet	100% (high)	5–6
1 × 454g/1lb packet	100% (high)	7–8

CANNED CORN KERNELS Drain off all but 2 tbsp of can juice. Place in a cooking dish with liquid. Cover and cook for time specified, stirring once.

Quantity	Power	Minutes
1 × 298g/10½oz can	100% (high)	2–3
1 × 340g/12oz can	100% (high)	2½–3

CREAMED CORN KERNELS Place in a cooking dish. Cover and cook for time specified, stirring once.

Quantity	Power	Minutes
1 × 298g/10½oz can	100% (high)	2–3
1 × 340g/12oz can	100% (high)	2½–3

Courgettes

FRESH Top and tail and slice thinly. Place in a shallow cooking dish with butter. Cover loosely and cook for the time specified, stirring once. Leave to stand, covered, for 2–3 minutes before serving.

Quantity	Butter	Power	Minutes
225g/8oz	25g/1oz	100% (high)	4–6½
450g/1lb	40g/1½oz	100% (high)	6–8

FROZEN Place in a shallow cooking dish with butter if liked. Cover loosely and cook for the time specified, stirring once Leave to stand, covered, for 2–3 minutes before serving.

Quantity	Butter	Power	Minutes
450g/1lb	40g/1½oz	100% (high)	7–8

Curly Kale

FRESH Remove the thick stalk and stems and shred. Place in a large dish with the water. Cover and cook for the specified time, stirring every 5 minutes. Leave to stand for 2 minutes before serving.

Quantity	Water	Power	Minutes
450g/1lb	150ml/¼ pint	100% (high)	15–17

F

Fennel

FRESH SLICED Place in a cooking dish with the water. Cover and cook for the time specified, stirring once. Leave to stand, covered, for 2–3 minutes before serving.

Quantity	Water	Power	Minutes
450g/1lb	3 tbsp	100% (high)	9–10

L

Leeks

FRESH WHOLE Trim and slit from the top of the white to the green leaves in 2–3 places. Wash thoroughly and place in a cooking dish with the water. Cover and cook for the time specified, rearranging twice. Leave to stand, covered, for 3–5 minutes before serving.

Quantity	Water	Power	Minutes
450g/1lb	3 tbsp	100% (high)	3–5
900g/2lb	5 tbsp	100% (high)	6–8

FRESH SLICED   Place in a cooking dish with the water. Cover and cook for the time specified, stirring once. Leave to stand, covered, for 2–3 minutes before serving.

Quantity	Water	Power	Minutes
450g/1lb	3 tbsp	100% (high)	8–10

FROZEN SLICED   Place in a cooking dish with the water. Cover and cook for the time specified, stirring once. Leave to stand, covered, for 2–3 minutes before serving.

Quantity	Water	Power	Minutes
225g/8oz	2 tbsp	100% (high)	6
450g/1lb	3 tbsp	100% (high)	11–12

M

Mangetout

FRESH   Trim and place in a cooking dish with the water. Cover and cook for the time specified, stirring once. Leave to stand, covered, for 2 minutes before serving.

Quantity	Water	Power	Minutes
100g/4oz	1 tbsp	100% (high)	3–4
225g/8oz	2 tbsp	100% (high)	4–5

FROZEN   Place in a cooking dish with the water. Cover and cook for time specified, stirring once.

Quantity	Water	Power	Minutes
1 × 200g/7oz packet	2 tbsp	100% (high)	3–4

Marrow

FRESH   Peel, remove seeds and cut into small neat dice. Place in a cooking dish without any water. Cover loosely and cook for the time specified, stirring once. Leave to stand, covered, for 2–3 minutes before serving.

Quantity	Power	Minutes
450g/1lb	100% (high)	7–10

FROZEN   To defrost only, place in a cooking dish, cover and cook for the time specified, stirring once. Drain and pat dry to use as required.

Quantity	Power	Minutes
225g/8oz	20% (defrost)	4–5
450g/1lb	20% (defrost)	9–10

Mixed Vegetables

FROZEN   Place in a cooking dish with the water. Cover and cook for the time specified, stirring once. Leave to stand, covered, for 2 minutes before serving.

Quantity	Water	Power	Minutes
225g/8oz packet	2 tbsp	100% (high)	4–5
450g/1lb packet	2 tbsp	100% (high)	7–8

Mushrooms

FRESH WHOLE   Trim and wipe mushrooms. Place in a cooking dish with water or butter. Cover and cook for the specified time, stirring twice. Leave to stand for 1–2 minutes before serving. Season to taste after cooking.

Quantity	Butter	or	Water	Power	Minutes
225g/8oz	25g/1oz		2 tbsp	100% (high)	3–4
450g/1lb	40g/1½oz		3 tbsp	100% (high)	4–5

FRESH SLICED   Trim, wipe and slice mushrooms. Place in a cooking dish with water or butter. Cover and cook for the specified time, stirring once. Leave to stand for 1–2 minutes before serving. Season to taste after cooking.

Quantity	Butter	or	Water	Power	Minutes
225g/8oz	25g/1oz		2 tbsp	100% (high)	2–3
450g/1lb	40g/1½oz		3 tbsp	100% (high)	3–4

FROZEN WHOLE BUTTON To thaw and cook, place in a shallow dish with a knob of butter. Cover and cook for the time specified, stirring twice. Season to taste to serve.

Quantity	Power	Minutes
100g/4oz	100% (high)	3–4
225g/8oz	100% (high)	5–6

O

Okra

FRESH Top and tail and sprinkle lightly with salt. Leave to drain for 30 minutes. Rinse and place in a cooking dish with the water or butter. Cover and cook for the time specified, stirring once. Leave to stand, covered, for 3 minutes before serving.

Quantity	Water	or	Butter	Power	Minutes
450g/1lb	2 tbsp		25g/1oz	100% (high)	8–10

Onions

FRESH WHOLE Peel and place in a cooking dish. Cover and cook for the specified time, rearranging and rotating once. Leave to stand, covered, for 2 minutes before serving.

Quantity	Power	Minutes
450g/1lb or 4 medium	100% (high)	10–12

FRESH SLICED Peel and cut into thin wedges or slices. Place in a cooking dish with the butter and water. Cover loosely and cook for the specified time, stirring once. Leave to stand, covered, for 5 minutes before serving.

Quantity	Butter	Water	Power	Minutes
450g/1lb	25g/1oz	2 tbsp	100% (high)	7–10

FROZEN WHOLE Place in a cooking dish with the water. Cover and cook for the time specified, stirring once. Leave to stand, covered, for 2–3 minutes before serving.

Quantity	Water	Power	Minutes
100g/4oz packet small whole	6 tbsp	100% (high)	2–3

FROZEN SLICES OR RINGS Place in a shallow dish, cover and cook for the time specified, stirring twice. Drain to use.

Quantity	Power	Minutes
225g/8oz	20% (defrost)	4–5
450g/1lb	20% (defrost)	8

P

Pak Soi (or Bok Choy Cabbage)

FRESH Slice stalks and leaves and place in a large dish so that the cabbage fits loosely. Add water, cover and cook for the time specified, stirring once. Leave to stand for 3–5 minutes before serving. Season after cooking.

Quantity	Water	Power	Minutes
450g/1lb	2 tbsp	100% (high)	6–8

Parsnips

FRESH WHOLE Peel and prick with a fork. Arrange in a large shallow dish with tapered ends to centre. Dot with butter and add water and lemon juice. Cover and cook for the time specified, rearranging once. Leave to stand, covered, for 3 minutes before serving.

Quantity	Butter	Water	Lemon juice	Power	Minutes
450g/1lb	15g/½oz	3 tbsp	1 tbsp	100% (high)	9–12

FRESH SLICES   Peel and slice. Place in a cooking dish with the butter and add water and lemon juice. Cover and cook for the time specified, stirring twice. Leave to stand, covered, for 3 minutes before serving.

Quantity	Butter	Water	Lemon juice	Power	Minutes
450g/1lb	15g/½oz	3 tbsp	1 tbsp	100% (high)	9–12

FRESH CUBES   Peel and cut into 1.5cm/½in cubes. Place in a cooking dish with the butter and add water and lemon juice. Cover and cook for the time specified, stirring twice. Leave to stand, covered, for 3 minutes before serving.

Quantity	Butter	Water	Lemon juice	Power	Minutes
450g/1lb	15g/½oz	3 tbsp	1 tbsp	100% (high)	9–12

FROZEN WHOLE   To thaw and cook. Arrange in a shallow dish with tapered ends to centre. Cover and cook for the time specified, rearranging once. Toss in butter and seasoning to serve.

Quantity	Power	Minutes
225g/8oz	100% (high)	7–8
450g/1lb	100% (high)	9–10

FROZEN SLICES   To thaw and cook. Place in a cooking dish, cover and cook for the time specified, stirring twice. Toss in butter and seasoning to taste to serve.

Quantity	Power	Minutes
225g/8oz	100% (high)	6–7
450g/1lb	100% (high)	12–14

FROZEN CUBES   To thaw and cook. Place in a cooking dish, cover and cook for the time specified, stirring twice. Toss in butter and seasoning to taste to serve.

Quantity	Power	Minutes
225g/8oz	100% (high)	4–5
450g/1lb	100% (high)	7–9

Peas

FRESH   Place in a cooking dish with butter and water. Cover and cook for the time specified, stirring once. Leave to stand, covered, for 3–5 minutes before serving.

Quantity	Butter	Water	Power	Minutes
100g/4oz	15g/½oz	2 tsp	100% (high)	3
225g/8oz	25g/1oz	1 tbsp	100% (high)	4–5
450g/1lb	50g/2oz	2 tbsp	100% (high)	6–8

FROZEN   Place in a cooking dish with water. Cover and cook for the time specified, stirring once. Leave to stand, covered, for 3 minutes before serving.

Quantity	Water	Power	Minutes
1 × 225g/8oz packet	2 tbsp	100% (high)	4–6
1 × 450g/1lb packet	4 tbsp	100% (high)	6–8

CANNED   Drain all but liquid specified. Place in a cooking dish with liquid. Cover and cook for time specified, stirring once.

Quantity	Liquid	Power	Minutes
1 × 283g/10oz can	1½ tbsp	100% (high)	1–2
1 × 425g/15oz can	2 tbsp	100% (high)	2–3

Peppers

TO BLANCH BEFORE STUFFING   Halve the peppers lengthways if liked or slice off tops to keep whole and remove and discard the seeds. Place in a shallow dish with the water, cover and cook for the time specified, rotating the dish once. Drain to use.

Quantity	Water	Power	Minutes
4 halves or 2 whole	2 tbsp	100% (high)	6–8

TO COOK RINGS OR SLICES FOR HOT SALADS, RICE MIXTURES
ETC   Core, seed and slice the peppers. Place in a dish with
the water, cover and cook for the time specified, stirring
once. Leave to stand, covered, for 5 minutes before using.

Quantity	Water	Power	Minutes
4	1 tbsp	100% (high)	5–7

FROZEN   Placed diced or sliced peppers in a bowl. Cover
and cook for the time specified, stirring twice. Drain to use.

Quantity	Power	Minutes
50g/2oz diced	20% (defrost)	1–1½
50g/2oz sliced	20% (defrost)	2
100g/4oz diced	20% (defrost)	2–2½
100g/4oz sliced	20% (defrost)	2½–3

FROZEN COOKED STUFFED   To thaw and reheat, stand
upright on a serving dish. Cover and cook for the time
specified, rearranging twice. Cover with foil and leave to
stand for 5 minutes before serving.

Quantity	Power	Minutes
2 whole stuffed	100% (high)	5
4 whole stuffed	100% (high)	10

Potatoes

MASHED OR CREAMED   Peel potatoes, cut into 1.5cm/½in
cubes and place in a cooking dish with water. Cover and
cook for the time specified, stirring once. Leave to stand,
covered, for 5 minutes. Drain and mash with butter and
seasoning to taste.

Quantity	Butter	Water	Power	Minutes
900g/2lb	25g/1oz	75ml/3fl oz	100% (high)	11–13

NEW OR OLD PEELED AND QUARTERED   Scrub new potatoes
and scrape if liked. Peel and quarter old potatoes. Place in
a cooking dish with the water. Cover and cook for the time

specified, stirring once. Leave to stand, covered, for 5 minutes before serving.

Quantity	Water	Power	Minutes
450g/1lb old	4 tbsp	100% (high)	7–10
450g/1lb new	4 tbsp	100% (high)	6–8

JACKET BAKED IN SKINS Scrub and prick skin. Place on a double sheet of absorbent kitchen towel. Cook for the time specified, turning over once. If cooking more than 2 potatoes arrange in a ring pattern. Leave to stand for 3–4 minutes before serving.

Quantity	Power	Minutes
1 × 175g/6oz	100% (high)	4–6
2 × 175g/6oz	100% (high)	6–8
3 × 175g/6oz	100% (high)	8–12
4 × 175g/6oz	100% (high)	12–15

SWEET Scrub and prick skin. Place on a double sheet of absorbent kitchen towel. Cook for the time specified, turning over once. Leave to stand for 5 minutes before using.

Quantity	Power	Minutes
450g/1lb	100% (high)	4–6

FROZEN NEW BOILED To thaw and reheat, place in a dish, cover and cook for the time specified, stirring twice. Leave to stand for 2 minutes before serving.

Quantity	Power	Minutes
225g/8oz	100% (high)	2½–3
450g/1lb	100% (high)	5–6

S

Spinach

FRESH   Chop or shred and rinse. Place in a dish without any additional water. Cover and cook for the specified time, stirring once. Leave to stand for 2 minutes before serving. Season to taste after cooking.

Quantity	Power	Minutes
450g/1lb	100% (high)	6–8

FROZEN (LEAF OR CHOPPED)   Place in a dish. Cover and cook for the specified time, stirring to break up twice during the cooking. Season to taste after cooking.

Quantity	Power	Minutes
1 × 275g/10oz packet	100% (high)	7–9

Swedes

FRESH   Peel and cut into 1.5cm/½in cubes. Place in a cooking dish with the water and butter. Cover and cook for the time specified, stirring twice. Leave to stand, covered, for 4 minutes. Drain and season to serve or mash with butter, cream and seasonings if liked.

Quantity	Butter	Water	Power	Minutes
450g/1lb	15g/½oz	2 tbsp	100% (high)	10–12

FROZEN CUBED   To thaw and cook, place in a cooking dish, cover and cook for the time specified, stirring twice. Toss in butter and seasonings or mash with butter, cream and seasonings if liked.

Quantity	Power	Minutes
225g/8oz	100% (high)	5–6
450g/1lb	100% (high)	8–10

Swiss Chard

FRESH Remove and discard the thick stalk and shred the leaves. Place in a large cooking dish with water. Cover and cook for the specified time, stirring every 3 minutes. Leave to stand for 2 minutes before serving. Season to taste after cooking.

Quantity	Water	Power	Minutes
450g/1lb	150ml/¼ pint	100% (high)	5½–6½

T

Tomatoes

TO PEEL FRESH Boil 750ml/1¼ pints water conventionally and place in a bowl. Add pricked tomatoes, cover and cook for the time specified. Remove with a slotted spoon, plunge into cold water – the skin will now peel away easily.

Quantity	Power	Minutes
Up to 450g/1lb	100% (high)	½

TO COOK WHOLE AND HALVES Prick whole or halve, arrange in a circle on a plate, cut sides up. Dot with butter and season with salt and pepper to taste. Cook for the time specified according to size and ripeness.

Quantity	Power	Minutes
1 medium	100% (high)	½
4 medium	100% (high)	2–2½
4 large (beef)	100% (high)	3½–4

Turnips

FRESH WHOLE Choose only small to medium turnips. Peel and prick with a fork. Arrange in a ring pattern in a large shallow dish. Dot with the butter and add water. Cover and cook for the time specified, rearranging once. Leave to stand, covered, for 3 minutes before serving.

Quantity	Butter	Water	Power	Minutes
450g/1lb	15g/½oz	3 tbsp	100% (high)	14–16

FRESH SLICES   Peel and slice. Place in a cooking dish with the butter and water. Cover and cook for the time specified, stirring twice. Leave to stand, covered, for 3 minutes before serving.

Quantity	Butter	Water	Power	Minutes
450g/1lb	15g/½oz	3 tbsp	100% (high)	11–12

FRESH CUBES   Peel and cut into 1.5cm/½in cubes. Place in a cooking dish with the butter and water. Cover and cook for the time specified, stirring twice. Leave to stand, covered, for 3 minutes before serving.

Quantity	Butter	Water	Power	Minutes
450g/1lb	15g/½oz	3 tbsp	100% (high)	12–14

Puddings and Desserts

Blackberry Fool

Serves: 4
Power setting: 100% (high)
Total cooking time: 4–5 minutes

450g/1lb blackberries, hulled
75g/3oz light muscovado sugar
juice of 1 small lemon
300ml/½ pint double cream
few blackberries to decorate

Place the blackberries, sugar and lemon juice in a bowl.
Cover and microwave at 100% (high) for 4–5 minutes,
until soft. Purée in a blender then pass through a fine sieve
to remove any seeds, and chill for 1 hour.

Whip the cream until it stands in stiff peaks. Fold in the
blackberry purée, blending well. Spoon into individual
dessert glasses and decorate with a few whole fresh
blackberries. Serve on the day of making.

Grapefruit Granita

Serves: 4
Power setting: 100% (high)
Total cooking time: 2–2½ minutes

juice of 1 large grapefruit
75g/3oz granulated sugar
2 tbsp brandy
300ml/½ pint rosé wine
1 grapefruit, peeled, pith removed and segmented
100g/4oz prepared soft fruit (strawberries, blackberries, raspberries or
    loganberries, for example)
few sprigs fresh lemon balm or mint to decorate

Place the grapefruit juice, sugar and brandy in a bowl. Cover
and microwave at 100% (high) for 2–2½ minutes or until
the sugar has dissolved, stirring twice. Leave to cool then
add the wine, blending well. Pour into a freezer tray and
freeze until firm, about 2–4 hours.

To serve, spoon the grapefruit granita into 4 chilled dessert glasses, shaving away the ice into thin slivers. Top each with a few grapefruit segments and with the soft fruit and decorate with the lemon balm or mint.

Serve at once.

Citrus Orange Charlotte

Serves: 6–8
Power setting: 50% (medium) and 100% (high)
Total cooking time: 4½ minutes

1 jam Swiss roll, cut into 15 slices
3 eggs, separated
100g/4oz castor sugar
4 oranges
175ml/6fl oz milk
1 tsp vanilla essence
15g/½oz powdered gelatine (or 2 tsp powdered agar-agar prepared according to packet instructions)
3 tbsp white wine
150ml/¼ pint double cream
orange segments and angelica leaves to decorate

Line a 1.2 litre/2 pint pudding basin with cling film then fill with the Swiss roll slices.

Whisk the egg yolks with the sugar until pale and creamy. Squeeze the juice from three of the oranges and peel, remove the pith and cut the remaining orange into segments. Add the orange juice, milk and vanilla essence to the egg yolk mixture, blending well. Microwave at 50% (medium) for 4 minutes, whisking well every 1 minute until the mixture starts to thicken and will coat the back of a wooden spoon – do not allow to boil and curdle.

Place the gelatine in a bowl with the wine and leave until spongy. Microwave at 100% (high) for ½ minute until clear and dissolved. Stir into the orange mixture and leave to cool.

Whisk the egg whites until they stand in stiff peaks. Fold into the orange mixture with the orange segments. Whip the cream until it stands in soft peaks and fold into the orange mixture. Pour into the prepared pudding basin and chill to set – about 2–4 hours.

To serve, invert on to a serving dish and remove the cling film. Serve decorated with orange segments and angelica leaves. Serve cut into thin wedges.

Blackcurrant Yogurt Creams

Serves: 4
Power setting: 100% (high)
Total cooking time: 3–3½ minutes

225g/8oz fresh blackcurrants, topped and tailed
100g/4oz light muscovado sugar
2 tbsp water
225g/8oz carton thick Greek yogurt
150ml/¼ pint double cream

Place the blackcurrants in a bowl with half of the sugar and the water. Cover loosely and microwave at 100% (high) for 3–3½ minutes until tender, stirring once. Allow to cool.

Divide the blackcurrants and their juice between 4 tall dessert glasses. Whip the cream until it stands in soft peaks. Fold in the yogurt and spoon over the blackcurrants. Sprinkle with the remaining sugar and chill for about 10 minutes to allow the sugar to dissolve slightly into the cream.

Serve with long-handled spoons to reach the fruit at the bottom.

Mini Pineapple Cheesecakes

Serves: 4
Power setting: 100% (high) and 50% (medium)
Total cooking time: 1½ minutes

25g/1oz butter or margarine
2 tsp golden syrup
100g/4oz gingernut, bran or digestive biscuits, crushed

175g/6oz Danish Buko full fat soft cheese with pineapple
5 tbsp whipping cream
220g/7oz can pineapple rings, well drained
angelica leaves to decorate

Place the butter in a bowl and microwave at 100% (high) for ½ minute to melt. Stir in the golden syrup and biscuit crumbs, blending well. Using a 7.5cm/3in biscuit cutter as a guide, make four biscuit bases on a greaseproof paper lined baking tray and refrigerate until set.

Place the cheese in a bowl and microwave at 50% (medium) for 1 minute to soften. Whip the cream until it stands in soft peaks then fold into the cheese mixture.

Carefully lift the biscuit bases on to individual serving plates. Spread two thirds of the cheese mixture over the bases. Top each with a pineapple ring. Place the remaining cheese mixture into a piping bag fitted with a large star-shaped nozzle and pipe a swirl of the mixture into the centre of each pineapple ring. Decorate with angelica leaves. Chill lightly before serving.

Orange Crème Brulées

Serves: 4
Power setting: 100% (high)
Total cooking time: 6–7 minutes

4 egg yolks
1 tbsp castor sugar
300ml/½ pint double cream
200ml/7fl oz single cream or milk
grated rind of 1 large orange
Topping:
4 tbsp demerara or castor sugar

Beat the egg yolks and castor sugar together until well blended. Stir in the creams and orange rind, blending well. Pour into 4 × 150ml/¼ pint ramekin dishes.

Stand in a dish filled with boiling water (checking that the level of the water is at the same height as the level of the orange mixture). Microwave at 100% (high) for 6–7 minutes or until the mixture starts to bubble, rearranging the ramekins once.

Leave until cool – the brulées will set upon cooling. Chill thoroughly for about 4–6 hours.

Sprinkle with the sugar and cook under a preheated hot grill until the sugar caramelizes. Cool then chill for at least 2 hours before serving.

Passion Fruit Cheesecake

Serves: 6–8
Power setting: 100% (high) and 50% (medium)
Total cooking time: 1½–1¾ minutes

100g/4oz digestive biscuit crumbs
50g/2oz butter
225g/8oz cream cheese
175g/6oz castor sugar
3 tbsp milk
3 eggs, separated
20g/¾oz agar-agar
6 tbsp grape or apple juice
150ml/¼ pint double cream
pulp of about 6 passion fruit

Line the base and sides of an 18cm/7in round tin with cling film. Place the butter in a bowl and microwave at 100% (high) for 1 minute. Add the biscuit crumbs and stir well to blend. Press evenly over the bottom of the prepared tin and chill to set, about 15 minutes.

Meanwhile, place the cream cheese in a bowl and microwave at 50% (medium) for ½–¾ minute to soften. Blend in 100g/4oz of the sugar, the milk and egg yolks. Dissolve the agar-agar in the grape or apple juice according to the packet instructions and whisk into the cheesecake mixture.

Whisk the egg whites until they stand in stiff peaks then whisk in the remaining sugar until thick and glossy. Fold

143

into the cheesecake mixture then pour over the biscuit crust. Chill until set, about 4 hours.

To serve, turn the cheesecake out on to a serving dish, removing the cling film carefully. Whip the cream until it stands in soft peaks. Spoon into a piping bag fitted with a large star-shaped nozzle and pipe whirls around the edge of the cheesecake. Spoon the passion fruit pulp into the centre.

Serve lightly chilled, cut into wedges.

Peach Melba Meringues

Serves: 4
Power setting: 100% (high) and 50% (medium)
Total cooking time: 4–5 minutes

2 tsp egg white, lightly beaten
100g/4oz icing sugar, sifted
50g/2oz plain chocolate
100g/4oz full fat soft cheese with peach melba
3 tbsp whipping cream
1 fresh peach, stoned and thinly sliced
a few fresh raspberries

Mix the egg white with the icing sugar to make a stiff mixture. Knead well to a smooth paste then divide and shape into 8 small balls. Place in a circle arrangement on a sheet of greaseproof paper and microwave at 100% (high) for 2–2½ minutes, or until well risen and crisp. Leave to stand for 5 minutes.

Break the chocolate into a bowl and microwave at 50% (medium) for 2–2½ minutes or until melted, stirring once. Drizzle over the meringues and leave to set.

Beat the cheese to soften. Whip the cream lightly with a fork then fold into the cheese mixture. Finely chop half of the peach slices and fold into the cheese mixture then use to sandwich pairs of the meringues together. Place each in a paper serving case if liked then top with the remaining peach slices and raspberries to decorate.

Serve as soon as possible.

Tropical Fruit Crumble

Serves: 4
Power setting: 100% (high)
Total cooking time: 6–8 minutes

175g/6oz wholemeal flour
100g/4oz unsweetened muesli
½ tsp baking powder
75g/3oz butter or margarine
50g/2oz soft brown sugar
425g/15oz can apricot halves in natural juice
2 passion fruit
1 banana, peeled and sliced
1 guava or mango, peeled, seeded or stoned and sliced

Mix the flour with the muesli and baking powder. Rub in the butter or margarine until the mixture resembles fine breadcrumbs then stir in the sugar.

Drain the apricots, reserving 6 tablespoons of the juice and place in a 1.2 litre/2 pint baking dish. Halve the passion fruit and scoop out the pulp. Spoon over the apricots. Add the bananas and guava or mango.

Cover with the crumble topping and microwave at 100% (high) for 6–8 minutes, giving the dish a quarter turn every 2 minutes. Leave to stand for 5 minutes before serving. Brown under a preheated hot grill if liked.

Serve hot or cold with soured cream or natural yogurt.

Lemon Baked Apples

Serves: 4
Power setting: 100% (high)
Total cooking time: 9–10 minutes

4 large cooking apples
50g/2oz stoned dates, chopped
4 tbsp lemon curd
4 tbsp demerara sugar
large knob of butter
8 tbsp water or apple juice

Wash and remove the cores from the apples and, using a sharp knife, score a cut around the middle of each to prevent bursting. Place in a cooking dish.

Meanwhile, mix the dates with the lemon curd and sugar and use to fill the apples. Dot with a little butter and pour the water or fruit juice around the apples. Microwave at 100% (high) for 9–10 minutes until tender and soft but not fallen, rearranging once. Leave to stand for 2 minutes before serving.

Cinnamon, Pear and Tofu Flan

Serves: 6
Power setting: 100% (high) and 50% (medium)
Total cooking time: 21–25½ minutes

75g/3oz butter or margarine
175g/6oz crunchy oat cereal
450g/1lb dessert pears, peeled, cored and sliced
grated rind and juice of 1 lemon
2 tbsp honey
1 tsp ground cinnamon
150g/5oz tofu
2 eggs, beaten
1 tbsp dark brown demerara sugar
1 dessert pear, cored and thinly sliced and tossed in 1 tbsp lemon juice

Place the butter in a bowl and microwave at 100% (high) for 1–1½ minutes to melt. Add the crunchy oat cereal and mix well to blend. Use to line the base of a 20cm/8in flan dish, pressing down well.

Place the pear slices, lemon rind and lemon juice in a bowl. Cover and microwave at 100% (high) for 6–8 minutes, until tender, stirring once. Allow to cool slightly then purée in a blender with the honey, cinnamon, tofu and eggs. Pour over the prepared crust and microwave, uncovered, at 50% (medium) for 14–16 minutes until set, giving the dish a quarter turn every 3–4 minutes. Sprinkle with the sugar and leave until cold.

When cold decorate the top of the flan with pear slices dipped in lemon juice. Serve lightly chilled, cut into wedges with natural yogurt if liked.

Wholewheat and Raisin Bread Pudding

Serves: 4
Power setting: 100% (high)
Total cooking time: 10–12 minutes

6 large slices wholewheat bread, crusts removed and halved
50g/2oz butter or margarine
50g/2oz raisins
3 eggs, beaten
3 tbsp brown sugar
few drops vanilla essence
425ml/15fl oz milk

Liberally spread the bread with the butter or margarine. Layer in a 1.5 litre/2½ pint dish with the raisins. Beat the eggs with the sugar and vanilla essence. Stir in the milk, blending well and pour over the bread mixture. Press down well and leave to stand for 3 minutes to allow the mixture to soak into the bread a little.

Place in a shallow dish of water and microwave at 100% (high) for 5–6 minutes. Leave to stand for 5 minutes. Microwave at 100% (high) for a further 5–6 minutes or until the bread pudding is almost set in the centre and firm around the edges. Leave to stand for 5 minutes. Brown and crisp under a preheated hot grill if liked before serving while hot.

Creamy Millet and Fruit Pudding

Serves: 4
Power setting: 100% (high) and 70% (medium high)
Total cooking time: 14½–16½ minutes

147

50g/2oz millet
170g/6oz can evaporated milk
400ml/14fl oz skimmed milk or water
25g/1oz demerara sugar
50g/2oz sultanas
25g/1oz dried apricots, snipped
25g/1oz chopped mixed peel
½ tsp ground nutmeg
a little milk or yogurt to serve

Place the millet, evaporated milk, milk or water, sugar, sultanas, half the apricots, mixed peel and nutmeg in a large bowl. Cover and microwave at 100% (high) for 4½ minutes, stirring twice.

Reduce the power setting to 70% (medium high) and microwave for 10–12 minutes, stirring three times, until smooth, creamy and cooked. Leave to stand, covered, for 10 minutes.

Serve hot, sprinkled with the remaining apricots and with a little milk or yogurt.

Tropical Crunch Crumble

Serves: 4
Power setting: 100% (high)
Total cooking time: 8–10 minutes

225g/8oz fresh pineapple, cubed
1 mango, peeled, stoned and cubed
2 oranges, peeled, pith removed and segmented
1 banana, peeled and sliced
2 eating apples, peeled, cored and cubed
1 tbsp lemon juice
3 pieces stem ginger, sliced
1 tbsp ginger wine or syrup
75g/3oz tropical mix muesli
75g/3oz wholemeal flour
75g/3oz butter or margarine
75g/3oz demerara sugar

Mix the pineapple with the mango, oranges, banana, apples, lemon juice, ginger and ginger wine or syrup, blending well. Spoon into a 1 litre/1¾ pint pie dish.

Mix the muesli with the flour. Rub in the butter or margarine and stir in the sugar. Spoon over the fruit mixture and level the surface. Microwave at 100% (high) for 8–10 minutes, giving the dish a quarter turn every 2½ minutes. Leave to stand for 5 minutes.

Brown under a preheated hot grill if liked. Serve hot with custard or cold with yogurt as liked.

Cider Poached Pears

Serves: 4
Power setting: 100% (high)
Total cooking time: 19–21½ minutes

200ml/7fl oz dry cider
50g/2oz castor sugar
juice of 1 lemon
4 large firm dessert pears
25g/1oz chopped mixed nuts
ice cream or smetana to serve

Place the cider, sugar and lemon juice in a deep heatproof bowl. Microwave, uncovered, at 100% (high) for 4–4½ minutes or until boiling, stirring twice.

Meanwhile, peel the pears leaving the stalks intact. Add to the lemon syrup and baste to coat thoroughly. Loosely cover and microwave at 100% (high) for 5–7 minutes, until just tender, turning over and rearranging twice. Remove with a slotted spoon and place in a serving dish.

Microwave the remaining syrup, uncovered, for a further 10 minutes or until thick and syrupy, stirring twice. Pour over the pears, cool then chill.

Serve the pears cold, basted with the syrup and sprinkled with the chopped nuts. Serve with ice cream or smetana.

Wholefood Baking

Wholewheat Loaf

Makes: 450g/1lb loaf
Power setting: 100% (high)
Total cooking time: 6½–7 minutes

1 tsp dried yeast
1 tsp castor sugar
300ml/½ pint warm water
450g/1lb wholewheat flour
½ tsp salt
15g/½oz butter or margarine
1 tbsp nibbed wheat, to sprinkle

Dissolve the yeast and sugar in 150ml/¼ pint of the water. Leave to stand until well risen and frothy, about 10–15 minutes.

Mix the flour with the salt in a bowl. Rub in the butter or margarine then add the yeast liquid and remaining water and mix to a firm but pliable dough. Knead, on a lightly floured surface until smooth and elastic, about 10 minutes. Return to the bowl, cover and leave to prove in a warm place until doubled in size, about 30 minutes. This process may be hastened in the microwave by giving the dough a brief burst of microwave energy – about 5 seconds occasionally, but caution must be exercised to prevent overheating (see page 24).

Knead the dough again briefly then shape to fit a 450g/1lb greased glass or microwave loaf dish. Cover and leave to prove again until the dough reaches the top of the dish. Sprinkle with the nibbed wheat and microwave at 100% (high) for 6½–7 minutes, giving the dish a quarter turn every 1½ minutes. Leave to stand for 5 minutes before turning out onto a wire rack to cool. If a brown crust is liked then the loaf may be placed under a preheated hot grill to crisp and brown after cooking in the microwave.

Oat-Topped Soda Bread

Makes: 675g/1½lb loaf
Power setting: 50% (medium) and 100% (high)
Total cooking time: 8 minutes

450g/1lb plain wholewheat flour
½ tsp salt
2 tsp bicarbonate of soda
50g/2oz butter or margarine
300ml/½ pint buttermilk
25g/1oz rolled oats

Mix the flour with the salt and bicarbonate of soda. Rub in the butter or margarine until the mixture resembles fine breadcrumbs. Bind together with the buttermilk to make a soft dough. Knead lightly and shape into a round cob. Place on a large greased plate and make a deep cross with a sharp knife on the top. Sprinkle with the rolled oats.

Microwave, without delay, at 50% (medium) for 5 minutes, giving the plate a half turn twice. Increase the power setting to 100% (high) and microwave for a further 3 minutes, giving the plate a half turn twice. Allow to stand for 10 minutes before transferring to a wire rack to cool.

Cheese and Walnut Scones

Makes: 8
Power setting: 100% (high)
Total cooking time: 2½–3 minutes

225g/8oz self-raising wholemeal flour
1 tsp baking powder
1 tsp mustard powder
25g/1oz butter or margarine
50g/2oz Cheddar cheese, grated
25g/1oz walnuts, finely chopped
150ml/¼ pint natural yogurt
2 tbsp milk

Mix the flour with the baking powder and mustard. Rub in the butter or margarine until the mixture resembles fine breadcrumbs. Stir in the cheese and walnuts, blending well. Add the yogurt and milk to mix to a soft dough.

Roll out on a lightly floured surface to about 2cm/¾cm thickness and stamp out 8 rounds using a 5cm/2in cutter.

Preheat a large browning dish according to the manufacturer's instructions, about 6 minutes at 100% (high). Lightly brush with a little oil, add the scones pressing down well. Microwave at 100% (high) for 2½–3 minutes, turning over once. Transfer to a wire rack to cool.

Granary Scone Whirl

Makes: 8 scones
Power setting: 100% (high)
Total cooking time: 3½–4 minutes

75g/3oz granary flour
75g/3oz wholewheat flour
50g/2oz plain white flour
½ tsp salt
3 tsp baking powder
50g/2oz butter or margarine
1 egg, beaten
5 tbsp milk
2 tbsp cracked wheat

Mix the flours with the salt and baking powder. Rub in the butter or margarine until the mixture resembles fine breadcrumbs. Add the egg and sufficient milk to bind to a soft dough. Knead lightly until smooth.

Base line an 18cm/7in round flan dish with greaseproof or silicone paper. Shape the dough into a round to fit the dish and pat gently into position. Mark into eight wedges with a sharp knife and sprinkle with the cracked wheat.

Microwave at 100% (high) for 3½–4 minutes, giving the dish a quarter turn every 1 minute. Leave to stand for 5 minutes before turning out on to a wire rack to cool.

Serve warm or cold with butter curls and preserve.

Danish Blue Ring

Makes: 8
Power setting: 100% (high)
Total cooking time: 3½–4 minutes

225g/8oz self-raising flour
1 tsp baking powder
50g/2oz butter or margarine
50g/2oz Danish Blue cheese, crumbled
150ml/¼ pint milk

Sift the flour with the baking powder into a bowl. Rub in the butter or margarine until the mixture resembles fine breadcrumbs. Add the cheese and stir in the milk to make a soft dough. Knead lightly until smooth.

Divide the mixture into eight equal pieces and form each into a ball. Base line a 20cm/8in round flan dish with greaseproof paper or silicone paper. Position the dough balls around the edge of the dish leaving the centre empty.

Microwave at 100% (high) for 3½–4 minutes, giving the dish a quarter turn every 1 minute. Leave to stand for 5 minutes then brown quickly under a preheated hot grill if liked. Remove from the dish and allow to cool on a wire rack.

Serve with butter, cheese or preserve.

Raisin Streusel Teabread

Makes: 10 slices
Power setting: 50% (medium) and 100% (high)
Total cooking time: 12–14 minutes

175g/6oz low fat soft cheese
175ml/6fl oz milk
8 tsp sunflower oil
6 tbsp clear honey
250g/9oz wholewheat flour
3 tsp baking powder

Filling:
100g/4oz raisins
50g/2oz walnuts, chopped
25g/1oz wheatgerm
1½ tsp ground cinnamon
2 tbsp maple syrup
Topping:
8 tsp maple syrup
25g/1oz wheatgerm
pinch of ground cinnamon

Lightly grease a 21.5 × 12cm/8½ × 4¾in loaf dish and line the base with greaseproof paper.

Mix the cheese with the milk, oil and honey, blending well. Sift the flour with the baking powder. Add to the milk mixture, blending well. Spread half of this mixture into the loaf dish, levelling carefully. Mix all the filling ingredients together and spread over the top. Cover with the remaining cake mixture and smooth the top.

Mix together the topping ingredients and spread over the cake mixture. Protect the ends of the loaf dish with 5cm/2in wide strips of foil. Place on an inverted saucer and microwave at 50% (medium) for 10 minutes, giving the dish a quarter turn every 2½ minutes. Remove the foil, increase the power setting to 100% (high) and cook for a further 2−4 minutes. The teabread will be cooked when it shrinks from the sides of the dish and no uncooked mixture can be seen through the bottom of the dish. Leave to stand for 10 minutes before turning out on to a wire rack to cool.

Serve warm or cold, cut into thin slices.

NOTE: To warm or reheat two slices of teabread, microwave at 100% (high) for ½−¾ minute.

Wholemeal Fruit Ring

Serves: 12
Power setting: 30% (low)
Total cooking time: 30−40 minutes

225g/8oz butter or margarine
175g/6oz soft brown sugar
3 tbsp creamed honey
250g/9oz wholemeal flour
1 tsp baking powder
2 tsp mixed spice
5 eggs, lightly beaten
900g/2lb mixed dried fruit
25g/1oz flaked almonds
50g/2oz glacé cherries, quartered
4 tbsp brandy or rum

Cream the butter or margarine with the sugar and honey
until fluffy. Sift the flour with the baking powder and spice,
adding the bran left in the sieve. Beat the eggs into the
creamed mixture, alternating with the flour to make a
smooth mixture. Fold in the fruit, almonds, cherries and
half of the brandy or rum, blending well.

Spoon into a well greased 30cm/12in glass or microwave
cake ring and microwave at 30% (low) for 30–40 minutes
or until a skewer or cocktail stick inserted into the centre of
the cake comes out clean of mixture, giving the cake a
quarter turn every 5 minutes. Leave to stand for 30 minutes
before turning out on to a wire rack to cool.

When cold pierce in several places with a fine skewer.
Sprinkle over the remaining brandy or rum and store in
an airtight tin for a few days to mature. Serve cut into slices.

High Tea Chocolate Loaf

Makes: 8–10 slices
Power setting: 50% (medium)
Total cooking time: 8½ minutes

100g/4oz butter or margarine
100g/4oz castor sugar
100g/4oz self-raising flour
2 eggs, beaten
2 tbsp drinking chocolate
2 tbsp cocoa powder
2 tbsp milk
1 tsp vanilla essence

Cream the butter or margarine with the sugar until light and fluffy. Add the flour and eggs, alternately to make a smooth mixture. Fold in the drinking chocolate, cocoa powder, milk and vanilla essence and blend well to mix. Spoon into a lightly oiled and greaseproof-paper lined 24 × 13 × 7cm/9½ × 5½ × 2¾in microwave loaf dish.

Microwave at 50% (medium) for 6 minutes. Position two 5cm/2in wide strips of foil at the ends of the loaf dish to shield the cake mixture and microwave at 50% (medium) for a further 2½ minutes until cooked. Leave to stand in the dish for 5 minutes before turning out on to a wire rack to cool.

Serve cut into thin slices.

Apricot and Carrot Cake

Serves: 8
Power setting: 50% (medium) and 100% (high)
Total cooking time: 11–12 minutes

175g/6oz carrots, peeled and grated
120ml/4fl oz sunflower oil
2 eggs, beaten
75g/3oz fructose or fruit sugar
75g/3oz unbleached plain white flour
1 tsp baking powder
1 tsp bicarbonate of soda
2 tsp ground cinnamon
75g/3oz no-need-to-soak dried apricots, chopped
45g/1½oz walnuts, chopped
Frosting:
75g/3oz low-fat soft cheese
1 tbsp creamed honey
1 tsp grated orange rind
toasted thread coconut to decorate

Grease and base line a 17cm/6¾in round cake dish with greaseproof paper.

Mix the carrots with the oil, eggs and fructose, blending well. Sift the flour with the baking powder, bicarbonate of soda and cinnamon. Fold into the egg mixture with the apricots and nuts, blending well. Spoon into the cake dish.

Place on an inverted plate and microwave at 50% (medium) for 9 minutes, giving the dish a quarter turn every 3 minutes.

Increase the power level to 100% (high) and cook for a further 2–3 minutes, giving the dish a quarter turn after 2 minutes, until well risen and cooked. Leave to stand for 10 minutes before turning out to cool on a wire rack.

To make the frosting, beat the cheese with the honey and orange rind. Swirl over the top of the cooled cake and sprinkle with a little toasted thread coconut.

Serve cut into thin wedges.

Crunchy Nut Gingerbread

Makes: about 12 squares
Power setting: 100% (high)
Total cooking time: 10–11½ minutes

225g/8oz wholemeal flour
½ tsp bicarbonate of soda
1 tbsp ground ginger
1 tsp ground mixed spice
4 tbsp mixed chopped nuts
100g/4oz butter or margarine
100g/4oz clear honey
1 tbsp molasses
100g/4oz muscovado sugar
150ml/¼ pint milk
2 eggs

Lightly grease and line the base of a 23 × 18cm/9 × 7in dish with greaseproof paper.

Sift the flour into a bowl, adding the bran left in the sieve. Add the bicarbonate of soda, ginger, mixed spice and nuts, blending well.

Place the butter or margarine and all but 1 teaspoon of the honey in a bowl with the molasses and sugar. Microwave at 100% (high) for 3 minutes, stirring once, until melted and well combined. Allow to cool slightly then stir in the milk and eggs, blending well.

Pour the egg mixture over the flour mixture and beat well to combine. Spoon into the prepared dish and place in the microwave on an upturned saucer or plate. Microwave at 100% (high) for 7–8½ minutes, giving the dish a quarter turn every 2 minutes. The gingerbread is cooked when it is springy to the touch and no wet or damp spots can be seen on the surface. Leave to stand for 10 minutes before turning out on to a wire rack to cool.

While still warm brush the remaining honey over the top of the gingerbread to give a shiny glaze.

Walnut and Bran Loaf

Makes: 10 slices
Power setting: 50% (medium)
Total cooking time: 12–14 minutes

100g/4oz muesli
25g/1oz bran
100g/4oz wheatmeal flour
2 tsp baking powder
½ tsp bicarbonate of soda
50g/2oz broken walnuts
150ml/¼ pint milk
150ml/¼ pint natural yogurt
1 egg
100g/4oz peeled carrots, grated
4 tbsp vegetable oil
50g/2oz muscovado sugar

Mix the muesli with the bran, flour, baking powder, bicarbonate of soda and three quarters of the walnuts, blending well.

Mix the milk with the yogurt, egg, carrots, oil and sugar. Add to the muesli mixture and beat well to blend. Spoon into a 22 × 12cm/9 × 5in loaf dish and sprinkle with the remaining walnuts. Shield the ends of the dish with 5cm/2in wide strips of foil. Place on an inverted saucer and microwave at 50% (medium) for 12–14 minutes, removing the strips of foil after 10 minutes, until cooked and the loaf shrinks from the sides of the dish, giving the dish a quarter turn every 3 minutes.

Leave to stand in the dish for 10 minutes before turning out on to a wire rack to cool. Serve cold buttered or with thin slices of cheese.

Cheesy Apricot and Raspberry Roulade

Serves: 6
Power setting: 100% (high) and 50% (medium)
Total cooking time: 5½–6½ minutes

Roulade:
175g/6oz low-fat soft cheese
50g/2oz castor sugar
2 large eggs, separated
45ml/9 tsp cornflour
pinch of salt
pinch of cream of tartar
castor sugar to sprinkle
Filling:
3 × 60g/2½oz cartons apricot fromage frais
100g/4oz raspberries, hulled
whipped cream and raspberries to decorate

Grease the base and sides of an 18 × 28cm/7 × 11in shallow baking dish. Line the base with oiled greaseproof paper.

Place the cheese in a bowl and microwave at 50% (medium) for ½ minute to soften. Blend in the sugar and eggs yolks then whisk in the cornflour and salt, until smooth.

Whisk the egg whites with the cream of tartar until they stand in stiff peaks. Fold into the cheese mixture with a metal spoon. Pour into the prepared dish and microwave at 100% (high) for 5–6 minutes, or until the centre of the roulade is still slightly tacky. Leave to stand for 2–3 minutes then turn out on to castor sugar coated greaseproof paper. Remove the lining paper and quickly trim the edges of the roulade to neaten. Roll up to enclose the greaseproof paper and leave until cold.

To make the filling, mix the fromage frais with the raspberries. Unroll the roulade and remove the paper. Spread with the raspberry mixture and roll up to enclose. Place on a serving plate and decorate with whirls of whipped cream and whole fresh raspberries.

Chill before serving, cut into slices.

One Cup Cookies

Makes: about 40
Power setting: 100% (high)
Total cooking time: 2 minutes

200ml/8fl oz muesli with tropical fruit
200ml/8fl oz self-raising flour
200ml/8fl oz light muscovado sugar
1 egg, beaten
125g/4½oz butter or margarine
chopped nuts or long-thread coconut (optional)

Mix the muesli with the flour, sugar, egg and butter or margarine, blending well. Divide and shape into about 40 small balls, about the size of a walnut. Roll in a few chopped nuts or coconut if liked.

Arrange half of the balls on a greased microwave baking tray, the microwave turntable or a large plate and microwave at 100% (high) for 1 minute. Allow to stand for 5 minutes then transfer to a wire rack to cool completely.

Repeat with the remaining biscuit mixture. Store in an airtight tin until required.

Lucy's Flapjacks

Makes: 8
Power setting: 100% (high)
Total cooking time: 4–4½ minutes

75g/3oz butter or margarine
40g/1½oz demerara sugar
175g/6oz rolled oats
1 tbsp golden syrup or honey

Place the butter or margarine in a bowl and microwave at 100% (high) for 1 minute to melt. Add the sugar, oats and honey or golden syrup and mix well to blend.

Spoon into a 23 × 18cm/9 × 7in shallow dish lined with cling film or greaseproof paper and level the surface. Microwave at 100% (high) for 3–3½ minutes, giving the dish a half turn after 1½ minutes. Using the back of a wooden spoon, press down the top of the flapjacks to firm. Leave to cool in the dish.

When cold cut the flapjacks into thick wedges with a sharp knife and remove from the dish to serve.

Entertaining Dishes

Speediest Ever Party Dip

Serves: 4–6
Power setting: 50% (medium)
Total cooking time: 1 minute

225g/8oz full-fat soft cheese with garlic
150ml/¼ pint natural yogurt
½ small green pepper, cored, seeded and finely chopped
1 tbsp snipped chives
salt and pepper
vegetable crudités to serve

Place the cheese in a bowl and microwave at 50% (medium) for 1 minute to soften. Add the yogurt and beat until smooth. Fold in the green pepper, chives and salt and pepper to taste. Turn into a small serving dish and chill.

Serve lightly chilled surrounded with a selection of vegetable crudités – cucumber strips, cauliflower florets, courgette discs, button mushrooms, carrot sticks or broccoli florets, for example.

Mushrooms and Peppers à la Grecque

Serves: 4
Power setting: 100% (high) and 50% (medium)
Total cooking time: 19–20 minutes

2 onions, peeled and finely chopped
1 red pepper, cored, seeded and sliced
1 green pepper, cored, seeded and sliced
1 yellow pepper, cored, seeded and sliced
1 tbsp fruity olive oil
120ml/4fl oz dry white wine
1 bouquet garni
225g/8oz button mushrooms, wiped
4 tomatoes, peeled, seeded and chopped
salt and pepper
2 tbsp chopped parsley
grated Parmesan cheese to garnish

Place the onions, peppers and oil in a bowl. Cover and microwave at 100% (high) for 4–5 minutes until softened, stirring once. Add the wine and bouquet garni, re-cover, reduce the power level to 50% (medium) and microwave for a further 5 minutes.

Add the mushrooms, tomatoes and salt and pepper to taste, blending well. Microwave, uncovered, at 50% (medium) for a further 10 minutes, stirring once. Remove and discard the bouquet garni, cover, cool then chill.

To serve, stir the parsley into the mushroom and pepper mixture. Spoon into a serving dish and dust with Parmesan cheese. Serve chilled with warm crusty bread.

Baked Quails' Eggs

Serves: 4
Power setting: 20% (defrost)
Total cooking time: 10–12 minutes

100g/4oz ready-made vegetable pâté
12 quails' eggs
120ml/4fl oz double cream
salt and pepper
parsley sprigs to garnish
toast fingers to serve

Spread the pâté evenly over the base of four lightly greased ramekins. Carefully crack three quails' eggs over the pâté in each dish and carefully puncture the yolks with the tip of a knife.

Spoon over the cream and season to taste with salt and pepper. Cover loosely with cling film and place in the microwave in a ring pattern. Microwave at 20% (defrost) for 10–12 minutes or until the eggs are just set.

Garnish with parsley sprigs and serve at once with crisp toast fingers.

Spicy Tomato Jellied Moulds with Devilled Sauce

Serves: 4
Power setting: 100% (high)
Total cooking time: ½ minute

300ml/½ pint tomato juice
1 tsp Worcestershire sauce
11g/0.4oz sachet powdered gelatine (or 2 tsp agar-agar prepared according to the packet instructions)
2 sticks celery, scrubbed and finely chopped
100g/4oz canned sweetcorn
3 hard-boiled eggs, shelled and chopped
salt and pepper
Sauce:
6 tbsp mayonnaise
2 tbsp whipped cream or thick set yogurt
1½ tbsp chopped parsley
2 tsp curry powder
1 tsp mango chutney
watercress sprigs to garnish

Place the tomato juice and Worcestershire sauce in a bowl, blending well. Remove 3 tablespoons to a small bowl and sprinkle over the gelatine. Leave until spongy then microwave at 100% (high) for ½ minute until clear and dissolved. Return to the tomato juice mixture and stir well to blend.

Add the celery, sweetcorn, eggs and salt and pepper to taste, blending well. Leave until almost set then spoon into four 150ml/¼ pint wetted moulds and chill until firm.

To make the sauce, mix the mayonnaise with the cream or yogurt, parsley, curry powder and mango chutney, blending well.

To serve, dip the moulds briefly into hot water then invert on to four small serving plates. Spoon over a little of the sauce and garnish with watercress sprigs.

Serve lightly chilled.

Brie, Cucumber and Yogurt Mousse

Serves: 6–8
Power setting: 100% (high) and 50% (medium)
Total cooking time: 1½–2 minutes

15g/½oz powdered gelatine (or 2 tsp powdered agar-agar prepared
  according to packet instructions)
150ml/¼ pint water
225g/8oz Blue Brie cheese, rinded
4 tbsp mayonnaise
1 tsp castor sugar
1 tsp lemon juice
salt and pepper
1 cucumber, peeled, seeded and grated
300ml/½ pint set natural yogurt
cucumber slices to garnish

Sprinkle the gelatine over the water in a bowl and leave
until spongy. Microwave at 100% (high) for ½–1 minute
until clear and dissolved. Allow to cool slightly.

Place the cheese in a bowl and microwave at 50%
(medium) for 1 minute until softened. Beat well until
smooth then add the mayonnaise, sugar, lemon juice and
salt and pepper to taste. Stir in the gelatine, cucumber and
yogurt, blending well.

Pour into a lightly oiled 1.2 litre/2 pint fluted ring mould
and chill until set.

To serve, dip the mould briefly into hot water then invert
on to a serving dish. Garnish with slices of cucumber and
serve with thin curls of Melba toast.

Blue Cheese and Calabrese Flan

Serves: 4–6
Power setting: 100% (high), 50% (medium) and 30% (low)
Total cooking time: 23½–25½ minutes

20cm/8in ready-cooked flan case or 175g/6oz shortcrust pastry
225g/8oz calabrese
3 tbsp water

100g/4oz Danish Blue cheese
3 eggs, beaten
150ml/¼ pint single cream
salt and pepper
¼ tsp ground nutmeg

If using pastry, roll out on a lightly floured surface to a round large enough to line the base and sides of a 20cm/8in flan dish. Press in firmly, taking care not to stretch. Cut the pastry away leaving a 5mm/¼in 'collar' above the dish to allow for any shrinkage. Prick the base and sides well with a fork. Place a double thickness layer of absorbent kitchen towel over the base, easing it into position round the edges. Microwave at 100% (high) for 3½ minutes, giving the dish a quarter turn every 1 minute. Remove the paper and microwave at 100% (high) for a further 1½ minutes.

To make the filling, place the calabrese and water in a bowl. Cover and microwave at 100% (high) for 3½ minutes. Drain and chop coarsely. Spread over the base of the cooked flan.

Place the cheese in a bowl and microwave at 50% (medium) for 1 minute to soften. Beat well then add the eggs, cream, salt and pepper to taste and nutmeg. Pour over the calabrese and microwave at 30% (low) for 14–16 minutes turning the dish every 3 minutes, or until just cooked and set in the centre.

Leave to stand for 10–15 minutes before serving warm with jacket baked potatoes and a tomato salad.

Egg-Fried Rice and Grains

Serves: 4
Power setting: 100% (high) and 50% (medium)
Total cooking time: 40½–41½ minutes

225g/8oz country rice and grain mix
600ml/1 pint boiling water or vegetable stock
15g/½oz butter or margarine
2 eggs, beaten

1 tbsp milk
salt and pepper
1 tsp Chinese five spice powder
2 tsp shoyu

Place the country rice and grains in a deep bowl with the boiling water or stock. Cover and microwave at 100% (high) for 3 minutes. Reduce the power level to 50% (medium) and microwave for a further 35 minutes, stirring twice, until the rice and grains are tender and the liquid has been absorbed. Leave to stand, covered, for 5 minutes.

Meanwhile, preheat a large browning dish according to the manufacturer's instructions, about 6 minutes at 100% (high). Add the butter or margarine and microwave at 100% (high) for a further ½ minute. Mix the eggs with the milk, salt and pepper to taste and Chinese five spice powder, blending well. Pour into the browning dish and microwave at 100% (high) for 1–2 minutes, beating every ½ minute until the egg is set and cooked.

Add the cooked rice and grain mixture with the shoyu and salt and pepper to taste, blending well. Microwave at 100% (high) for 1 minute to reheat. Serve hot with curry-style or Chinese dishes.

Honeyed Bean, Corn and Potato Salad

Serves: 4
Power setting: 100% (high)
Total cooking time: 6–8 minutes

450g/1lb new potatoes, scrubbed
4 tbsp water
205g/7oz can red kidney beans, drained
198g/7oz can sweetcorn kernels, drained
small bunch spring onions, trimmed and chopped
1 tbsp chopped parsley
Dressing:
2 tsp wholegrain mustard
1 tbsp wine vinegar
4 tbsp sunflower oil

1 tsp clear honey
salt and pepper

Place the potatoes in a bowl with the water. Cover and microwave at 100% (high) for 6–8 minutes, stirring once. Leave to stand, covered, for 5 minutes then slice thickly and leave to cool.

Mix the potatoes with the beans, sweetcorn, spring onions and parsley in a serving bowl.

To make the dressing, mix the mustard with the vinegar, oil, honey and salt and pepper to taste, blending well. Pour over the salad ingredients and toss well to coat. Serve as soon as possible.

Greek Feta and Vegetable Casserole

Serves: 4–6
Power setting: 100% (high)
Total cooking time: 41 minutes

225g/8oz long-grain rice
550ml/18fl oz boiling water
2 × 283g/10oz packets frozen casserole vegetables
6 tbsp cold water
1 tbsp chopped fresh herbs
4 tbsp tomato purée
283g/10oz packet frozen cut leaf spinach
250ml/8fl oz natural yogurt
2 egg yolks
1 tbsp cornflour
1 tbsp French mustard
225g/8oz Feta cheese, cubed
salt and pepper

Place the rice in a large cooking dish with the boiling water. Cover loosely and microwave at 100% (high) for 3 minutes. Reduce the power setting to 50% (medium) and microwave for a further 12 minutes, stirring twice. Leave to stand, covered, for 5 minutes, then fluff with a fork to separate.

Meanwhile, place the frozen vegetables in a bowl with the cold water. Cover and microwave at 100% (high) for 10

minutes, stirring once. Drain well then stir in the herbs and
tomato purée, blending well.

Place the spinach in bowl, cover and microwave at 100%
(high) for 8 minutes, stirring twice. Drain well then stir
into the rice.

Place the vegetables in the base of a large cooking dish.
Cover with the rice and spinach mixture. Mix the yogurt
with the egg yolks, cornflour and mustard, blending well.
Fold in the cheese and salt and pepper to taste. Spoon over
the rice and microwave at 100% (high) for 8 minutes or
until the mixture is just set around the edges of the dish.
Leave to stand for 5 minutes before serving with a crisp
seasonal salad.

Fruit and Vegetable Rajah

Serves: 4
Power setting: 100% (high)
Total cooking time: 17–19 minutes

1 tbsp sunflower oil
2 red onions, peeled and sliced
½ head celery, scrubbed and sliced
1 tbsp plain flour
1 tbsp hot Madras curry powder or own blend of curried spices
200ml/7fl oz hot vegetable stock
pinch of ground ginger
pinch of garam masala
grated rind and juice of 1 lemon or lime
2 bananas, peeled and thickly sliced
50g/2oz raisins
50g/2oz sultanas
4 medium dessert apples, peeled, cored and quartered
400g/14oz can apricot halves, peach slices or mango slices, drained
150ml/¼ pint soured cream or yogurt
1 tbsp chopped coriander leaves

Place the oil, onion and celery in a large cooking dish. Cover
and microwave at 100% (high) for 5–7 minutes, stirring
once, until tender but still crisp. Add the flour and curry

powder, blending well. Microwave at 100% (high) for 1 minute, stirring once.

Gradually add the stock, ginger, garam masala and lemon or lime rind and juice, blending well. Microwave at 100% (high) for 3 minutes, stirring every 1 minute to keep the sauce smooth.

Add the bananas, raisins, sultanas, apples and apricots, peach slices or mango slices, blending well. Cover and microwave at 100% (high) for 8 minutes, stirring twice, until tender but not fallen.

Swirl the soured cream or yogurt into the vegetable and fruit mixture and sprinkle with the coriander to serve. Serve with a rice or grain accompaniment and a selection of pickles or chutneys.

Jamaican Rice and Beans

Serves: 4
Power setting: 100% (high) and 50% (medium)
Total cooking time: 52–57 minutes

175g/6oz red kidney beans, soaked
boiling water
175g/6oz creamed coconut, grated
2 tbsp vegetable oil
1 large onion, peeled and chopped
2 garlic cloves, peeled and crushed
2 red peppers, cored, seeded and chopped
225g/8oz American long-grain rice
225g/8oz tomatoes, peeled and chopped
few drops of Tabasco sauce
salt and pepper
4 spring onions, trimmed and chopped

Place the soaked beans in a cooking dish. Cover with boiling water, cover and microwave at 100% (high) for 10 minutes. Reduce the power setting to 50% (medium) and microwave for a further 20–25 minutes, adding extra boiling water to cover if needed. Drain and set aside.

Meanwhile, place the coconut in a jug and pour over

enough boiling water to make up to 60ml/1 pint. Stir well to dissolve and blend.

Place the oil in a bowl with the onion and garlic. Cover and microwave at 100% (high) for 3 minutes, stirring once. Add the peppers, cover and microwave at 100% (high) for a further 2 minutes. Add the rice and stir well to blend.

Add the tomatoes, Tabasco, salt and pepper to taste, the coconut milk and a further 150ml/¼ pint of boiling water. Cover and microwave at 100% (high) for 3 minutes. Reduce the power setting to 50% (medium) and microwave for a further 12 minutes, stirring once. Stir in the cooked red kidney beans and microwave at 100% (high) for 2 minutes. Leave to stand, covered, for 5 minutes.

Fluff the rice and beans carefully with a fork and serve hot, sprinkled with the chopped spring onions. Serve with a vegetable salad.

Mama Mia's Italian Aubergine and Pasta Mould

Serves: 4
Power setting: 100% (high)
Total cooking time: 43 minutes

175g/6oz wholemeal pasta shells
900ml/1½ pints boiling water
675g/1½lb aubergines
1 large onion, peeled and finely chopped
1 garlic clove, peeled and crushed
2 carrots, peeled and finely chopped
2 tbsp vegetable or olive oil
2 × 425g/15oz cans chopped tomatoes
1 tsp dried oregano
salt and pepper
100g/4oz mushrooms, wiped and sliced
1 yellow pepper, cored, seeded and chopped
2 courgettes, trimmed and sliced
75g/3oz vegetarian hard cheese, grated
chopped parsley to garnish

Place the pasta in a bowl with the boiling water. Cover and microwave at 100% (high) for 12 minutes, stirring once. Drain thoroughly and set aside.

Prick the aubergines with a fork and remove the stalks. Microwave at 100% (high) for 4 minutes. Leave to stand for 5 minutes then slice thinly crossways. Line the base and sides of a 2.4 litre/4 pint round dish or bowl with two-thirds of the aubergine slices.

Place the onion, garlic, carrots and oil in a dish. Cover and microwave at 100% (high) for 10 minutes, or until the vegetables are tender, stirring twice. Add the tomatoes, oregano and salt and pepper to taste, blending well. Cover and microwave at 100% (high) for 5 minutes, stirring once. Purée in a blender.

Stir the mushrooms, yellow pepper and courgettes into half of the sauce. Cover and microwave at 100% (high) for 5 minutes. Stir in the cooked pasta and cheese, blending well. Spoon into the aubergine lined mould and top with the remaining aubergine slices. Cover and microwave at 100% (high) for 5 minutes. Leave to stand, covered, for 5 minutes before inverting on to a serving dish.

Reheat the remaining tomato sauce mixture at 100% (high) for 2 minutes. Spoon a little over the aubergine mould and sprinkle with chopped parsley to garnish.

Slice into thick wedges to serve with a crisp seasonal salad.

All Seasons Crespella

Serves: 4
Power setting: 100% (high)
Total cooking time: 17½–22 minutes

450g/1lb spinach, chopped or shredded and washed
1 onion, peeled and chopped
1 garlic clove, peeled and crushed
15g/½oz butter or margarine
350g/12oz ricotta or cottage cheese
1 tbsp double cream
pinch of ground nutmeg

salt and pepper
8 thin slices mozzarella cheese
8 ready-cooked pancakes or crêpes
Sauce:
25g/1oz butter or margarine
25g/1oz flour
300ml/½ pint milk
4 tbsp grated Parmesan cheese

Place the spinach in a bowl without any additional water. Cover and microwave at 100% (high) for 6–8 minutes, stirring once. Leave to stand while cooking the onion.

Place the onion, garlic and butter or margarine in a bowl. Cover and microwave at 100% (high) for 3 minutes, stirring once. Add the ricotta or cottage cheese, cream, nutmeg, drained spinach and salt and pepper to taste, blending well.

Place an equal quantity on to each pancake and top with a slice of mozzarella cheese. Roll up and place, seam-side down, in a large shallow dish.

To make the sauce, place the butter or margarine in a jug and microwave at 100% (high) for 1 minute. Blend in the flour and milk and microwave at 100% (high) for 3½–4 minutes, stirring every 1 minute until smooth, boiling and thickened. Season to taste with salt and pepper and spoon over the pancakes to coat evenly. Sprinkle with the Parmesan cheese and microwave at 100% (high) for 4–6 minutes, or until hot, cooked and bubbly.

Brown under a preheated hot grill if liked. Serve hot with a crisp green salad.

Kiwi Fruit Ice Cream

Serves: 8
Power setting: 100% (high)
Total cooking time: 2–3 minutes

100g/4oz light muscovado sugar
150ml/¼ pint water
6 ripe kiwi fruit, peeled and coarsely chopped

juice of 1 lemon
4 eggs
300ml/½ pint single cream
150ml/¼ pint double cream
kiwi fruit slices to decorate

Place the sugar and water in a bowl and microwave at 100%
(high) for 2–3 minutes, or until the sugar has dissolved,
stirring three times. Add the lemon juice and allow to cool.

Place the kiwi fruit, lemon juice mixture, eggs and creams
in a blender and purée until smooth. Pour into a freezer
tray and freeze until half-frozen, about 1 hour. Return to
the bowl and whisk until smooth and any ice crystals have
been broken down. Pour back into the freezer tray and freeze
until firm, about 2–4 hours.

Serve scooped into chilled dessert glasses decorated with
a few slices of kiwi fruit.

Grapefruit, Fromage Frais and Ginger Wedges

Serves: 6–8
Power setting: 100% (high) and 50% (medium)
Total cooking time: 4½ minutes

75g/3oz butter or margarine
175g/6oz oat or ginger biscuits, crushed
Filling:
135g/4¾oz packet grapefruit and orange jelly
200ml/7fl oz water
225g/8oz cream cheese
100g/4oz plain or apricot fromage frais
150ml/¼ pint soured cream
2 eggs, separated
Topping:
1 grapefruit, peeled, pith removed and cut into segments
25g/1oz demarara sugar
1 tbsp chopped glacé or stem ginger

Place the butter or margarine in a bowl, cover and
microwave at 100% (high) for 1½ minutes to melt. Stir
in the biscuit crumbs and mix well to coat. Use to line the

base of a 20cm/8in loose-bottomed cake or deep flan tin. Chill to set.

Place the jelly cubes in a bowl with the water. Microwave at 100% (high) for 2 minutes, then stir well to dissolve.

Place the cream cheese in a bowl and microwave at 50% (medium) for 1 minute to soften. Stir in the fromage frais, jelly, soured cream and egg yolks, blending well. Whisk the egg whites until they stand in stiff peaks and fold into the cheese mixture with a metal spoon. Pour over the prepared base and chill until set.

To serve, remove the dessert from the tin and place on a serving plate. Decorate with the grapefruit segments rolled in sugar and the chopped ginger. Serve lightly chilled cut into wedges.

Yogurt Tangs with Orange Peppercorn Sauce

Serves: 4
Power setting: 100% (high)
Total cooking time: 4½ minutes

4 oranges
50g/2oz sugar
15g/½oz powdered gelatine (or 2 tsp powdered agar-agar prepared
    according to packet instructions)
4 tbsp boiling water
250g/8oz thick Greek yogurt, drained
150ml/¼ pint double cream
Sauce:
juice of 2 oranges
2 tbsp clear honey
1–2 tbsp Grand Marnier
½–1 tsp pink peppercorns, crushed
crisp dessert biscuits to decorate

Lightly oil and base-line four 7.5cm/3in diameter dishes with greaseproof paper. Finely grate the rind from 1 orange and squeeze the juice from three. Place the orange juice and rind in a bowl, add the sugar and microwave at 100% (high) for 3 minutes, stirring twice. Allow to cool.

Dissolve the gelatine in the boiling water and whisk well into the cool orange mixture. Fold in the yogurt, blending well.

Whip the cream until it stands in soft peaks and fold into the yogurt mixture.

Remove the rind and white pith from the remaining orange and cut into 4 slices. Place a slice in the base of each prepared ramekin dish. Spoon over the orange yogurt mixture and chill to set.

To make the sauce, place the orange juice and honey in a bowl and microwave at 100% (high) for 1½ minutes. Stir in the Grand Marnier and pink peppercorns, blending well. Leave to cool.

To serve, invert the yogurt tangs on to individual serving dishes. Spoon over or surround with the sauce. Decorate with crisp dessert biscuits just before serving.

Shimmering Real Orange Jelly

Serves: 4–6
Power setting: 100% (high)
Total cooking time: 4 minutes

6 large oranges
100g/4oz castor sugar
4 tbsp white wine
4 tbsp water
20g/¾oz powdered gelatine (or 2½ tsp powdered agar-agar prepared
    according to packet instructions)
5 tbsp boiling water
3 tbsp Cointreau or other orange liqueur
sliced kiwi fruit to decorate

Grate the zest from 2 of the oranges and squeeze the juice from all 6. Place the orange juice, orange zest, sugar, wine and water in a bowl and microwave at 100% (high) for 4 minutes or until the sugar has dissolved, stirring every 1 minute.

Dissolve the gelatine in the boiling water and stir into the orange mixture with the liqueur, blending well. Leave until thick and almost set then pour into a 750ml/1¼ pint wetted jelly mould. Chill to set firm, about 4–6 hours or overnight.

To serve, dip briefly into hot water then invert on to a serving plate. Decorate with slices of kiwi fruit and serve as soon as possible.

Redcurrant and Raspberry Yogurt Ice

Serves: 4
Power setting: 100% (high)
Total cooking time: 6–7 minutes

450g/1lb redcurrants, topped and tailed
100g/4oz brown sugar
2 tbsp water
300ml/½ pint low-fat raspberry yogurt
150ml/¼ pint double cream
100g/4oz fresh wholemeal breadcrumbs
25g/1oz icing sugar
15g/½oz flaked almonds
2 eggs, separated
1 tbsp Kirsch
4 tsp glycerine
red food colouring (optional)
2 tsp arrowroot powder

Place the redcurrants in a bowl with the sugar and water, blending well. Cover loosely and microwave at 100% (high) for 5 minutes, stirring once. Leave to stand for 5 minutes before draining, reserving the juice.

Whisk the yogurt with the cream until lightly thickened. Fold in the redcurrants, breadcrumbs, icing sugar, almonds, egg yolks, Kirsch, glycerine and colouring if liked.

Whisk the egg whites until they stand in stiff peaks and fold into the redcurrant mixture with a metal spoon. Pour into a 1.5 litre (2½ pint) freezer proof container, cover and freeze until firm.

Meanwhile blend the reserved juice with the arrowroot and microwave at 100% (high) for 1–2 minutes until clear and thickened, stirring every ½ minute. Add a little water to thin the sauce if necessary.

Serve the ice cream scooped into chilled glasses with the warm or cold sauce.

Apple and Cinnamon Cheesecake

Serves: 8
Power setting: 100% (high)
Total cooking time: 7½–9½ minutes

Base:
225g/8oz digestive biscuits, crushed
1 tsp ground cinnamon
50g/2oz butter
Filling:
450g/1lb cooking apples, peeled, cored and chopped
1 tsp ground cinnamon
50g/2oz soft brown sugar
juice of ½ lemon
225g/8oz cream cheese
225g/8oz tub Greek yogurt
15g/½oz powdered gelatine
2 tbsp cold water
Topping:
225g/8oz tub Greek yogurt
50g/2oz sugar
2 drops of vanilla essence
1 tsp ground cinnamon

To make the base, mix the digestive biscuit crumbs with the cinnamon, blending well. Place the butter in a small bowl and microwave at 100% (high) for 1 minute to melt. Add to the digestive biscuit mixture, blending well. Press into a greased 20cm/8in loose-bottomed flan tin and chill to set.

To make the filling, place the apples, cinnamon, sugar and lemon juice in a bowl. Cover and microwave at 100% (high) for 6–8 minutes, until tender, stirring once. Purée in a blender or pass through a fine sieve. Beat the cream cheese with the yogurt and apple purée. Sprinkle the gelatine over the water in a small bowl and microwave at 100%

(high) for ½ minute until clear and dissolved. Stir into the apple mixture, blending well then pour over the biscuit crust. Chill until set.

To make the topping, mix the yogurt with the sugar and vanilla essence, blending well. Remove the cheesecake from the tin and place on a serving plate. Swirl the yogurt topping over the cheesecake and sprinkle with the cinnamon to decorate. Serve chilled and cut into wedges.

Truffled Coconut and Mango Chocolate Loaf

Serves: 6
Power setting: 100% (high) and 50% (medium)
Total cooking time: 5½–7¼ minutes

350g/12oz fresh mango, chopped
4 tbsp brown rum
few drops vanilla essence
100g/4oz butter or margarine
175g/6oz creamed coconut
200g/7oz plain dessert chocolate
200g/7oz digestive, macaroon or ginger biscuit crumbs
Mango rum cream:
300ml/½ pint double cream
1 tbsp dark rum
1 tbsp mango juice

Lightly oil and base-line a 900g/2lb loaf tin with greaseproof paper. Place the mango in a bowl with the rum and vanilla essence, mixing well. Cover and leave to marinate for at least 2 hours.

Place the butter and creamed coconut in a bowl and microwave at 100% (high) for 2½–4 minutes until melted. Place the chocolate in a bowl and microwave at 50% (medium) for 3–3¼ minutes until melted, stirring twice. Mix the chocolate with the coconut mixture and the biscuit crumbs, blending well. Drain the marinade from the mango and stir into the biscuit mixture. Fold in the mango, mixing well.

Spoon into the prepared tin and level the surface. Cover and chill to set, about 8 hours.

Meanwhile to prepare the mango rum cream, place the cream, rum and mango juice in a bowl and whip until it stands in soft peaks. Chill lightly.

Serve the loaf cut into thin slices with a mound of fluffy mango rum cream.

Liqueur-soaked Muesli Trifle

Serves: 6
Power setting: 100% (high)
Total cooking time: 7–8 minutes

100g/4oz sugar
300ml/½ pint apple juice
225g/8oz cherries, stoned
100g/4oz raspberries, hulled
100g/4oz strawberries, hulled
2 peaches, peeled, stoned and sliced
100g/4oz blackcurrants or redcurrants, topped and tailed
3 tbsp Beaume de Venise wine, Kirsch or cherry brandy
200g/7oz muesli
300ml/½ pint thick natural yogurt
150ml/¼ pint peach or strawberry fromage frais
mint leaves and toasted nuts to decorate

Place the sugar and apple juice in a heatproof bowl and microwave at 100% (high) for 4–5 minutes, stirring 3 times.

Add the cherries, raspberries, strawberries, peaches and currants, blending well. Cover and microwave at 100% (high) for 3 minutes until lightly softened but not fallen, stirring once. Drain thoroughly, reserving the juice. Stir in the Beaume de Venise, Kirsch or cherry brandy, blending well.

Place the muesli in the base of a serving dish and sprinkle over the liqueur-flavoured syrup. Top with the poached fruits. Chill thoroughly.

Spoon over the natural yogurt to cover, trickle over the

fromage frais and, using the tip of a knife, swirl to marble the mixtures together. Decorate with mint leaves and toasted nuts. Serve chilled.

Frothy Chocolate Cups

Serves: 4
Power setting: 50% (medium)
Total cooking time: 2½–3 minutes

1 egg, separated
2 tbsp apricot extra jam
225g/8oz plain dessert chocolate
2 tbsp brandy
150ml/¼ pint double cream
225g/8oz quark
75g/3oz icing sugar, sifted
4 ready-made plain chocolate shells or cups

Mix the egg yolk with the jam, blending well. Grate half of the chocolate and stir into the egg mixture with the brandy.

Whip the cream until it stands in soft peaks. Fold all but 2 tablespoons into the brandy mixture with the quark. Whisk the egg white until it stands in stiff peaks. Whisk in the icing sugar until thick and glossy. Fold into the brandy mixture with a metal spoon and pour into the chocolate shells.

Break the remaining chocolate into a bowl and microwave at 50% (medium) for 2½–3 minutes, stirring once until melted. Stir in the reserved cream, blending well. Drizzle over the chocolate filled shells or cups and chill thoroughly before serving.

St Clement's Sabayon

Serves: 4
Power setting: 100% (high) and 30% (low)
Total cooking time: 2½–3 minutes

100g/4oz castor sugar
4 egg yolks
1 tsp cornflour
finely grated rind and juice of 1 large orange
3 tbsp lemon juice
To decorate:
powdered cocoa
langue de chat biscuits

Place the sugar, egg yolks, cornflour and orange rind in a
bowl and whisk until very thick and creamy. Whisk in the
orange and lemon juice and microwave at 100% (high) for
1–1½ minutes until hot, but not cooked or set. Whisk
again to blend well, then reduce the power to 30% (low)
and microwave for 1½ minutes.

Whisk for about 4 minutes until the mixture becomes very
thick and will leave a trail on the surface when lifted. Pour
into warm dessert glasses and sprinkle with powdered cocoa.

Serve warm or cool, within one hour, with langue de chat
biscuits.

Index

Carol Bowen
A–Z of Microwave Cookery £2.99

Whether you want to thaw meat, cook frozen peas, ripen cheese or melt chocolate, you can save time by using your microwave.

Carol Bowen, an expert in microwave cookery, has spent years testing basic items which are suitable for cooking the microwave way. The result is the *A–Z of Microwave Cookery*, now fully revised and expanded to cover almost 200 basic foods, arranged alphabetically from almonds to yogurt.

Information is at your fingertips with a useful glossary of terms, a guide to temperature settings, and precise instructions on:

Preparing food for the oven
Covering, turning or stirring during cooking
Power settings and cooking times according to weight

The indispensable at-a-glance guide to fast, efficient cooking.

Combination Microwave Cookery £2.99

With a Combination Microwave Oven you can have the best of conventional convection cooking and grilling with the benefits of a microwave – all in one appliance.

Now *combination microwave cookery* offers a guidebook to help you make the most of this sophisticated new form of cooking.

Combination Microwave Cookery is the first truly comprehensive book of its kind. It's packed with mouth-watering recipes covering all food types from roasts to potatoes, fish to pastries, and meals for every occasion. But it's also a thorough guide to the range of combination microwave ovens, their characteristics and operation.

All model types are covered, and there is a simple chart to help you tailor recipes to your particular appliance.

All Pan books are available at your local bookshop or newsagent, or can be ordered direct from the publisher. Indicate the number of copies required and fill in the form below.

Send to: **CS Department, Pan Books Ltd., P.O. Box 40, Basingstoke, Hants.   RG21 2YT.**

or phone: 0256 469551 (Ansaphone), quoting title, author and Credit Card number.

Please enclose a remittance* to the value of the cover price plus: 60p for the first book plus 30p per copy for each additional book ordered to a maximum charge of £2.40 to cover postage and packing.

*Payment may be made in sterling by UK personal cheque, postal order, sterling draft or international money order, made payable to Pan Books Ltd.

Alternatively by Barclaycard/Access:

Card No.

Signature:

Applicable only in the UK and Republic of Ireland.

While every effort is made to keep prices low, it is sometimes necessary to increase prices at short notice. Pan Books reserve the right to show on covers and charge new retail prices which may differ from those advertised in the text or elsewhere.

NAME AND ADDRESS IN BLOCK LETTERS PLEASE:

Name

Address

3/87

Carol Bowen
A–Z of Microwave Cookery £2.99

Whether you want to thaw meat, cook frozen peas, ripen cheese or melt chocolate, you can save time by using your microwave.

Carol Bowen, an expert in microwave cookery, has spent years testing basic items which are suitable for cooking the microwave way. The result is the *A–Z of Microwave Cookery*, now fully revised and expanded to cover almost 200 basic foods, arranged alphabetically from almonds to yogurt.

Information is at your fingertips with a useful glossary of terms, a guide to temperature settings, and precise instructions on:

Preparing food for the oven
Covering, turning or stirring during cooking
Power settings and cooking times according to weight

The indispensable at-a-glance guide to fast, efficient cooking.

Combination Microwave Cookery £2.99

With a Combination Microwave Oven you can have the best of conventional convection cooking and grilling with the benefits of a microwave – all in one appliance.

Now *combination microwave cookery* offers a guidebook to help you make the most of this sophisticated new form of cooking.

Combination Microwave Cookery is the first truly comprehensive book of its kind. It's packed with mouth-watering recipes covering all food types from roasts to potatoes, fish to pastries, and meals for every occasion. But it's also a thorough guide to the range of combination microwave ovens, their characteristics and operation.

All model types are covered, and there is a simple chart to help you tailor recipes to your particular appliance.

All Pan books are available at your local bookshop or newsagent, or can be ordered direct from the publisher. Indicate the number of copies required and fill in the form below.

Send to: **CS Department, Pan Books Ltd., P.O. Box 40, Basingstoke, Hants. RG21 2YT.**

or phone: 0256 469551 (Ansaphone), quoting title, author and Credit Card number.

Please enclose a remittance* to the value of the cover price plus: 60p for the first book plus 30p per copy for each additional book ordered to a maximum charge of £2.40 to cover postage and packing.

*Payment may be made in sterling by UK personal cheque, postal order, sterling draft or international money order, made payable to Pan Books Ltd.

Alternatively by Barclaycard/Access:

Card No. ☐☐☐☐☐☐☐☐☐☐☐☐☐☐☐☐☐☐☐

Signature:

Applicable only in the UK and Republic of Ireland.

While every effort is made to keep prices low, it is sometimes necessary to increase prices at short notice. Pan Books reserve the right to show on covers and charge new retail prices which may differ from those advertised in the text or elsewhere.

NAME AND ADDRESS IN BLOCK LETTERS PLEASE:

....

Name———————————————————————————

Address———————————————————————————

—————————————————————————————

—————————————————————————————

—————————————————————————————

3/87